Edward Cline

ROUTING ISLAM

I0414212

Essays from My Cartridge Pouch

PATRICK HENRY PRESS

Library of Congress Cataloguing-in-Publication Data

Edward Cline (1946 -)
Routing Islam, Edward Cline

ISBN-13: 978-1539426868
ISBN-10: 1539426866
ASIN: B01MECMMJ2

Cover and Title Page: Battle of Abu Klea, Sudan (January 1885), by William Barnes Wollen (1857-1936); painting date, unknown
Back Cover: Portrait of the author by Roxanne Albertoli

Patrick Henry Press
Waco, TX

NONFICTION

The New Sparrowhawk Companion

Letters of Marque

Islam's Reign of Terror

A Handbook on Islam

Corsairs & Freebooters

Running Out My Guns

Broadsides in the War of Ideas

From the Crow's Nest

Routing Islam

Boarding Parties & Grappling Hooks

Rational Scrutiny: Paradoxes and Contradictions in Detective Fiction

Contents

Foreword by the Author

This is a collection of my most recent columns on Rule of Reason and edwardcline.blogspot.com., chiefly on the subject of Islam's incursions on the West and especially in the United States. The incursions are made possible mainly at the invitation of corrupt, cravenly cowardly, and reality-denying *dhimmis* in Europe and in America. Other guilty parties have as their conscious goal the subjugation and destruction of the West.

Not all of the essays discuss or are even remotely related to Islam. I have included a handful of pieces on political correctness and the decrepit state of our culture. There really isn't that much anymore that can be regarded as "good news" or encouraging.

Blue and underlined terms are links to relevant articles. Those reading this volume on Kindle may be able to read the links.

Edward Cline
Waco, Texas
October 2016

Friday, October 07, 2016

Chapter 1: Let's Slander the "Prophet"!

Let's start with Obama saying it a first time: "The future must not belong to those who slander the prophet of Islam." He said this in Cairo on June 4, 2009, and then again at the UN in September 2012.

And Attorney General Loretta "Hang 'em High" Lynch has promised to pursue "hate speech," aka "blasphemy," "slandering the prophet," or otherwise mocking all things Islamic.

The signs, in code, say "Uphold Freedom of speech!"

It's so easy to mock Islam, to defame the "religion," to kick it in the butt as its faithful bow to Mecca, moon the West, and do the "gimme gimme gimme" gesture with their hands, and bang their heads on the ground (doing that ritual Islamic dance, the *Shahada*, which is not quite the "Twist" or the "Macareni").

Attorney General Loretta "Hang 'em High" Lynch:
The Premier Sharia Enforcer, CAIR's best ally, and
a Muslim's best friend outside of a mosque.

The 20th century *salat*, or the ritual bowing in homage, can be performed in various stances, such as standing up preferably on one foot, but has been modified to incorporate bobbing and weaving. Hip Muslims found the traditional posture boring and not very lively. "As much of the ground must be felt by the nose as the forehead. The elbows are raised and the palms are on level with either the shoulders or the ears, with fingers together. Toes must not have lint or dirt between them, and must not wiggle." Many young Muslims regarded the tradition posture "degrading."

Did you know that if you rearrange the letters in Islam, you can make a SALAMI sandwich! Well, almost. You'd need an extra "A."

Did you know that the town of Walla Walla was actually founded by Muslim settlers in 1818, but not before the local Nez Perce Indians had been subdued and made to submit, paying *wampum* as *jizya*. Those who refused to abjure Wontonka, the local god, and swear to Allah, were summarily beheaded.

So, what is an Islamic martyr going to do with 72 raisins? One option is to emulate Carol in *The Walking Dead* and make a cookie casserole.

How long would a fight last between a Norwegian and a Muslim (ethnic identity immaterial)? No time at all. Muslims fight only in gangs. As they do just about everything else. The Muslim would be joined by other Muslims. Muslims are not really men. They can't stand alone.

Doing the "Salah," in a Saudi parking lot, without a backwards baseball cap, which is *de rigueur* with "hip" Muslims. Hip Muslims will often start doing the "*wudu* booty call" after performing the "gimme gimme gimme."

They need their brothers to help them do their dirty work. Individual bullying is an alien concept to most Muslims, except for "lone wolves," who are known to try being Mr. Macho all by themselves. But while committing what infidels call a "crime," a Muslim prefers to do it with other Muslims, to form a bond of "Brotherhood." That way, if they are ever arrested, they can share the blame and martyrdom.

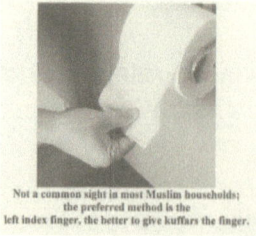

Not a common sight in most Muslim households;
the preferred method is the
left index finger, the better to give kuffars the finger.

Bidets were not invented by the racist French, but by Muslims who did not like returning to the dinner table from the bathroom with recently busy and soiled left hands. But Muslims had to wait a long, long time before one of them invented the bidet. His name was Mohammad, he was a French-Algerian Muslim, and a former member of the Paris *Pompiers*. While helping his colleagues hose down burning Citroens set on fire by fellow Muslims protesting that the sky was blue, he had a brainstorm. And then he was declared an apostate. He had a thought. Thoughts are verboten. But he went ahead and endured the banishment.

Let's take a look at some of those <u>72 virgins</u> promised to martyrs.

In addition to Quranic translations of 78:33 specifying the virgins will be <u>voluptuous</u>[20], Sahih International translates it as *"full-breasted [companions] of equal age"*. Tafsir al-Jalalayn says *"and **buxom** maidens (kawā'ib is the plural of kā'ib) of equal age (atrāb is the plural of tirb)"*. Several Islamic scholars explain that they will have *"**large, round breasts** which are not inclined to hang"*.[21]
These houris will have:

- Wide and beautiful/lovely eyes
- Eyes like pearls (or marbles)
- Be hairless except the eye brows and the head (no makeup, no hair styling)

In addition to Quranic translations of 78:33 specifying the virgins will be <u>**voluptuous**</u>, Sahih International translates it as *"full-breasted [companions] of equal age"*. Tafsir al-Jalalayn says *"and **buxom** maidens (kawā'ib is the plural of kā'ib) of equal age (atrāb is the plural of tirb)"*. Several Islamic scholars explain that they will have *"**large, round breasts** which are not inclined to hang."*

All of these virgins will be:

- Beautiful (depends on your definition; beautiful by Renaissance standards?)
- White skinned (will be as European-looking as possible,
- Muslim males, regardless of their ethnic origins, seem to prefer White Chocolate to Brown or Black
- (African, Asian or Mideastern   woman need not apply)
- 60 cubits [27.5 meters] tall (nickname "Big Bertha")
- 7 cubits [3.2 meters] in width (or Plus Size, unless she's on Curves)
- Transparent to the marrow of their bones (not a pretty sight, raw marrow)
- Eternally young (on the Avon program)
- Companions of equal age (to avoid jealousies and rivalries)

- Also, there are other very important attributes to these perfect mannequins. They will be:

- Chaste
- Restraining their glances (naturally shy)
- Have a modest gaze (downcast eyes, looking at his or her

feet)
- Splendid (be a good conversationalist, be able to discuss Plato's Forms)
- Pure (as the driven snow?)
- Non-menstruating / non-urinating/ non-defecating and child-free (just like Eve)
- Never be dissatisfied (she wouldn't dare!)
- Will sing praise (with the voice of Tiny Tim)

I think there was a movie that dramatized some of these virgins. I think it was the original *West World*.

Cultural enrichment illustrated

Let's touch on the subject of that special contribution of Islamic hegemony: *Cultural enrichment*. Women in Sweden and Germany are being told to just submit to rape by Muslims, it's their duty, it's their chance to sacrifice themselves to gang rape, and beatings, and disfigurement. It's the patriotic thing to do! Never mind the risks of pregnancy, of contracting incurable diseases the Muslims bring from their "homelands." If you wind up looking like a leper, that's the price you must pay to be a loyal, true Swede or German. Become enriched! Let him whisper sweet nothing in your ear! Before he bites it off! And slashes your face with a razor!

And here's a consolation thought: Boys and men who rape together, pray together. There's an element of piety in all of us. Don't be so judgemental!

Watch your tongue! Do not call the invasion of your country by Somalis, Afghans, Turks, Iraqis, and Syrians, and other creatures a form of the Bubonic plague! You can be fined and even jailed for uttering such a thing!

Moonies and Muslims share a tradition of mass marriages; But Mohammad did not believe in polygamy. The more wives the merrier, and the younger the better.

Now, Mohammad was a big fan of child brides. He married several children himself by the time he was a crotchety, middle-aged horny toad. An "age of consent" was an alien concept, a "downer." He could hardly wait to fondle a child that that had yet to leave its manger. And often he fondled them when they were still in the manger. (Cradles hadn't yet been invented.) Uncle Mo was a pedophile. He loved children. Perhaps even boys.

But it does no good to call him a pedophile, just as it does no good to call him a rapist, a murderer, a thief, a bandit, an inventor of genocide, a consumer of widows he made by chopping off the heads of their husbands. All these labels are to Muslims but virtues, of beatific lettuce bespangling his military tunic, of brilliant feathers in his turban. These are things to strive to be in the ordinary Muslim. Uncle Mo is the model, ideal man to emulate.

What other Muslim can be portrayed as a Christ-like saint, as a brilliant military strategist, as a dignified "lawgiver," as a humble "man of peace"? He is seen as being those things by quaking Western *dihimmis*, by career blankers-out-of-reality. Mohammad's rap sheet belies all those appellations. He is "untouchable." He may not be slandered, nor should his "religion" be slandered.

Attorney General Lynch can try to do her worst to gag and punish purveyors of "hate speech" (except for hate-spewing Muslims). The Rodham creature can threaten to shut down all manner of freedom of speech over the Internet. CAIR can litigate in our compliant judicial system.

To me, ISIS and the Muslim Brotherhood can go shoe a goose. Americans who want to scuttle the First Amendment are traitors.

Three cheers for Islamophobia!

https://edwardcline.blogspot.com/2016/10/lets-slander-prophet.html

Saturday, December 5, 2015

Chapter 2: Eyes Wide Shut: Political Correctness and Islam

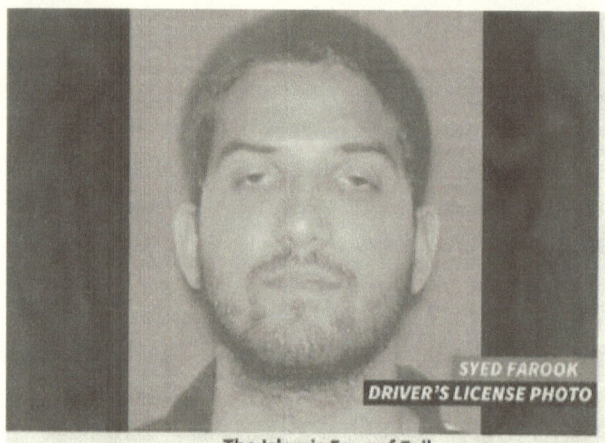

SYED FAROOK
DRIVER'S LICENSE PHOTO

The Islamic Face of Evil

Remember that "Attack Watch" slogan of Obama's near the end of his first term, "If you see something, say something," when he was trying to get Americans to inform on other Americans who were vocally critical of him? In this case, Syed Farook's neighbors saw something, but didn't say anything, for fear of being labeled racists or Islamophobes or profilers.

Stephanie Condon wrote in a CBS report in September 2011, "Conservatives mock Obama's 'AttackWatch.com,":

Anticipating a nasty fight in 2012, President Obama's re-election campaign on Tuesday launched a site, called AttackWatch.com , designed to push back against attacks on the president's record.

> "We all remember the birth certificate smear, the GOP's barrage of lies about the Affordable Care Act, and the string of other phony attacks on President Obama that we've seen over the past few years," Jim Messina, Obama for America's campaign manager, wrote in an email to the president's supporters. "There are a lot of folks on

the other side who are chomping at the bit to distort the President's record. It's not a question of if the next big lie will come, just when -- and what we're prepared to do about it."

Yet so far, the site seems to have been most effective at giving conservatives more ammunition against the president. Conservative blogger Michelle Malkin is referring to the initiative as the "snitch police squad", while the conservative site Human Events is calling it the "little brother initiative." The Drudge Report, the news aggregating site popular among conservatives, features a link to AttackWatch.com under the headline, "See something, say something," in reference to the Department of Homeland Security's public awareness campaign.

Its "public awareness campaign" to the contrary notwithstanding, the DHS has done its bit in frightening Americans to not "say something," being one of the biggest vehicles of politically correct thought and speech. And Redlands neighbors' not "saying something" worked out very well, to Barack Obama's benefit. It allowed him to dig up that hoary old chestnut, "workplace violence," and also to grandstand again for more gun controls.

Had these neighbors the courage to notify law enforcement authorities about the frequent presence of Middle Eastern-looking strangers in the vicinity and the unusual activities at Farook's house, the San Bernardino terrorist attack would not have occurred. The police would have found the arsenal of weapons and pipe bombs in Farook's house. They would have pulled up the DHS's record of Farook's comings and goings. They would probably have found the packaging those weapons and materials came in. They might have learned the true identity of Farook's "wife," and where she actually came from.

They would have discovered, not the makings of a neighborhood Tupperware party, but the preparations for another major Islamic jihadist attack.

All that might have happened had not many Americans been intimidated by the MSM and the White House and the PC police into "not saying something" to the authorities.

On one hand, one can't blame them for not speaking up. How many Americans today want to risk being painted with the "racist," "Islamophobe," "bigot" brush, and often to their own detriment? How many of them could afford the legal representation to counter the smears?

Another Islamic Face of Evil,
Tashfeen Malik, Farook's wife

On the other hand, how many of them have allowed their minds to shut down, to allow their freedom of speech to be abridged by the risk of inviting slurs and character assassination? To shut down one's mind is an act of volition, of choice. How many of them see what they see yet contemplate it with "eyes wide shut" – that is, seeing the evidence before their eyes yet denying or suppressing its reality and significance? How many are guilty of refusing to acknowledge reality, the facts, and the truth?

Caroline Glick, in her Jerusalem Post column of December 3rd, "Column One; America's pathological denial of reality," asked:

How much lower will America sink before it regains its senses? Wednesday, two Muslims walked into a Christmas party at a community service center in San Bernardino, California where one worked. They were wearing body armor and video cameras and carrying automatic rifles, pipe bombs and pistols. They opened fire, killed 14, and wounded 17.

The murderers, Syed Farook and his wife, Tashfeen Malik were killed by police.

Speaking to the *Daily News*, Farook's father said his son, "was very religious. He would go to work, come back, go to pray, come back. He's Muslim." Farook's neighbor told the paper that over the past two years, Farook exchanged his Western dress for Islamic gowns and grew a beard.

These data points lead naturally to the conclusion that Farook and his wife were jihadists who killed in order to kill in the name of Islam.

But in America of December 2015, natural conclusions are considered irresponsible, at best.

Farook's neighbor ought to have reported the transformation to the authorities. He didn't. He was unable or unwilling to follow those "data points" to a conclusion. He could only sense where they could lead to. Possibly he was afraid of immediate repercussions, of personal recrimination if it turned out that Farook *wasn't* up to no good. Just because Farook was looking more and more like a standard, unassimilated Muslim and less like one who was well-adjusted to American standards, apparently wasn't good enough a reason to take action.

I have few occasions or reasons to quote Franklin D. Roosevelt, but there is one thing he said early in his first inaugural address in 1933, a statement whose sentiment applies today as well as it did eighty-two years ago. The sentiment has always stuck in my mind because it intrigued me.

This great Nation will endure as it has endured, will revive and will prosper. So, first of all, let me assert my firm belief that the only thing we have to fear is fear itself—nameless, unreasoning, unjustified terror which paralyzes needed efforts to convert retreat into advance.

Fear of something can cause one to not take action against that something. Fearful indecision can emasculate one's capacity for action against that which causes one's fear.

It took the FBI a few days, but it finally decided that reality trumps fantasy and the denial of enemy action, and that the Farook/Malik attack on the San Bernardino Inland Regional Center was indeed a terrorist attack. The Washington Post reported on November 4th in its column "San Bernardino attacker pledged allegiance to Islamic State leader, officials say":

> One of the two people involved in the San Bernardino attack that killed 14 people pledged allegiance to the leader of the Islamic State, the clearest indication yet that this was an act of terrorism, according to two law enforcement officials.

The *clearest indication*? Isn't that evidence enough? It's just an *indication*, which together with all the other evidence proves an attack by Islamic jihadists, with or without ISIS's endorsement or sanction? I keep picturing our *dhimmified* FBI putting its finger to the wind to determine which way it's blowing. How scientific, how technologically advanced! You aren't allowed to think "Islam," but in the end, you must think "Islam." Thinking and not-thinking of something can only lead to the destruction of one's mind. We see that in the fancy epistemological dance steps our authorities are taking. But reality is merciless and won't let you get away with *not* seeing. *A* cannot be *A* and *non-A* at the same time.

> Since the massacre Wednesday — which also wounded 21 people — officials have scrambled to determine whether they were looking at a terrorist attack or an extremely unusual and lethal case of *workplace violence*. They have also revealed that the attackers had amassed an arsenal of explosives and ammunition, suggesting the possibility of further violence. [*Italics* mine.]

Workplace violence? That bewilderingly evasive, politically correct, and obscene, cowardly term "popularized" by Janet Napolitano when she was head of the DHS, on the occasion of the Fort Hood massacre by Nidal Hasan? After all, Farook and Malik entered Farook's "workplace" and proceed to do violence against its employees. Ergo, it was "workplace violence"! (Actually, the term has a long history, and has gone by other names, so she didn't coin it, strictly speaking. She merely revived it, which caused ongoing mockery of her and of the term.)

The official said the FBI was perplexed in the days after the attack and was still searching for clues that would indicate radicalization on the part of either one.

There's Islam, the "peaceful" religion. And then there's "radicalized" Islam. There's the "peaceful" Islam which calls for killing Jews, enslaving or killing non-Muslim infidels, in the name of Allah, commanded by Mohammad. And then there's "radicalized" Islam, which calls for killing Jews, enslaving or killing non-Muslim infidels, in the name of Allah, commanded by Mohammad. We mustn't confuse the two, you see. It's so easy to be "perplexed" about a motive. However, you can no more "radicalize" Islam than you can find the square root of one.

You can't be "radicalized" by Islam unless you are open to committing violence, not unless you have a simmering urge to kill that's repressed but screaming to get out. You can't be "radicalized" by a nihilistic "religion" unless there's a kernel of nihilism in you already, nurtured by Islam.

> "The FBI is chasing down any contacts these two may have had and whether those contacts are indicative of radicalization or external plotting or are purely incidental," said Rep. Adam B. Schiff (Calif.), the ranking Democrat on the House Intelligence Committee.

> The congressman said the shooting did not appear to be "an act of spontaneous workplace violence." But, he said, it could have been the culmination of a longer-term grievance.

What a priceless understatement: The massacre could have been "the culmination of a longer-term grievance"! Such as a hatred of the West, of America, of life itself? No, the congressman and his ilk in the MSM and law enforcement refuse to entertain that impolitic possibility. They wouldn't want to appear to be bigoted against Islam.

In the meantime, Attorney General Loretta Lynch wasted no time inveighing against, not the killers, but "anti-Muslim rhetoric." I am assuming that this and my other columns over the years about Muslims and Islam qualify as "anti-Muslim rhetoric." I call it freedom of speech. I call it identifying evil and expounding on why it thrives in this country and why Islam has no place in America. Lynch delivered her remarks at the 10th anniversary celebration of the founding of Muslim Advocates, which, like the Muslim Brotherhood and Hamas-connected Council on American Islamic Relations (CAIR), is a purported Muslim civil rights organization.

Attorney General Lynch: "Edging" towards censorship

Pamela Geller of Atlas Shrugs, in her December 4th article, "Attorney General Loretta Lynch: 'Actions Predicated On Violent Talk' Toward Muslims 'Will Be Prosecuted,'" reported on Lynch's barely-disguised warning to those who engage their freedom of speech to warn against the depredations of Islam. Drawing on BuzzFeed's account of Lynch's address to the Muslim Advocates, she wrote:

> "My message not just to the Muslim community but to all Americans is 'We cannot give in to the fear that these backlashes are really based on,'" Lynch said.

Geller: What backlashes? Americans have been slaughtered at a Christmas party in the cause of Allah. This is Sharia enforcement. This is sedition by the Obama administration. This should not be the response of the wholesale slaughter of American "unbelievers."

> Speaking at Muslim Advocate's 10th anniversary dinner, the attorney general said, "We cannot give in to the fear that these backlashes are really based on." Speaking at Muslim Advocate's 10th anniversary dinner, Lynch said since the terrorist attacks in Paris last month, she is increasingly concerned with the "incredibly disturbing rise of anti-Muslim rhetoric … that fear is my greatest fear."

Disturbing anti-Muslim rhetoric? Where? In the streets? At home? Oh, that's right. On blog spots like Geller's and Robert

Spencer's and Daniel Greenfield's and a dozen more, including my own. Or in the statements of political candidates. Her greatest fear is not about possibly being gunned down by Muslims in combat gear at *her* Christmas party. And she isn't much concerned about the victims in Paris or the victims in San Bernardino. Her sympathy rests with the alleged victims of that "anti-Muslim backlash," a "backlash" that never actually materializes.

Following the Paris attacks, there has been an uptick in violent attacks on Muslims and threats against mosques across the country. That, combined with heated political rhetoric such as GOP presidential front runner Donald Trump's call to register Muslim Americans, has Muslim community leaders worried that they could be facing a new era of discrimination.

Lynch made it clear that she shares those concerns, but vowed to use the DOJ to protect Muslims from discrimination and violence. Noting the rise in violence against Muslims and mosques in the wake of the Paris attacks, Lynch added that, "When we talk about the First amendment we [must] make it clear that actions predicated on violent talk are not American. They are not who we are, they are not what we do, and **they will be prosecuted."**

So, by "predication," is Lynch saying that if someone reads my column and goes out and smears a mosque door with pig's blood, or gives a Muslim the finger on a public street, my "violent talk" – what a contradiction! Talk isn't "violent, it has no metaphysical power to hurt anyone, except perhaps their 'feeling'" – he could be arrested and charged with a hate crime, and I could be charged with "hate speech"? See the video of Lynch pontificating on "violent talk" here, courtesy of the Daily Wire.

Has she anything to say about the "violent talk" or "anti-infidel rhetoric" that can be found on various Internet social media that can "radicalize" the Farooks and Maliks of America and which "predicates" *their* violence? Probably not.

I wonder what she would make of this. IPT's John Rossomando reported on December 4th that

> On Thursday a leading ISIS propagandist who tweets under the handle Muslimah congratulated Farook and Malik for the San Bernardino assault, calling them martyrs.

> "May Allah Accept Our Brother & Sister who were martyred after carrying out an operation against Crusaders in USA," she tweeted.

I'll bet you didn't know that people with disabilities and in wheelchairs attending a Christmas party were "Crusaders." But if you're not surprised, it means that you know that Islamic jihadists regard civilians and non-combatants and even children as legitimate targets, just as Jews are in Israel and everywhere else.

> "What is greatly concerning to us is the rise, I remember 9/11 and those were very disturbing days, I heard some disturbing things from people that I never thought I would hear (Video appears to have been edited at this point to remove something Lynch said) the rise of the internet, the ability of people to issue hateful speech of all types from the anonymity of a screen obviously increases that hateful rhetoric," she added.

> "Now obviously this is a country that is based on free speech, but when it edges towards violence, when we see the potential for someone lifting that mantle of anti-Muslim rhetoric... when we see that, we will take action."

Lynch is "edging towards" committing the violence of government censorship. This should not surprise anyone. Obama nominated her as a soul-mate who would fit his political agenda, and she was Attorney General Eric Holder's first choice of successor in that office.

Daniel Greenfield, in his FrontPage article of December 4th, "Attorney General Tells Muslim Pro-Terrorists She Will Crack Down on Anti-Muslim Rhetoric," not only noted everything in Geller's column, but also some interesting information about the head of the Muslim Advocates.

> Muslim Advocates, headed by Farhana Khera, who peppered a smiling Lynch with questions about "anti-Muslim rhetoric", had played a significant role in crippling DOJ investigations of Islamic terrorism by eliminating training materials about Islamic terrorism.
>
> Khera had vocally opposed the sorts of sting operations that had succeeded in capturing a number of ISIS terror plotters before they were able to act. A similar sting might have stopped the San Bernardino massacre. She had opposed the FBI recruiting informants and supported Muslim leaders linked to terrorism. She had even defended terror charities like the Holy Land Foundation.
>
> And she and another Muslim Advocates figure had urged Muslims not to provide information to the FBI. "Any information you provide to the FBI can be used as the basis for further surveillance and investigation of your community," a Muslim Advocates lawyer had said. "So you really don't want to be putting yourself in a situation where you're providing anybody with information about people in your community that the FBI is now gonna follow up and start investigating those people."

Loretta Lynch, Farhana Khera, and Tashfeen Malik – a "Band of Sisters" and enemies of America, united in their resolve to punish "thoughtcrime," "hate speech," and "Islamophobia," and any other kind of thought and speech they can think of. As long as it can be throttled and prohibited by Sharia law. Political correctness is one of Islam's most effective allies.

Political correctness is a destructive censoring power itself. One can choose to censor oneself, or it can be imposed on one by an external "authority." It demands that we see without seeing – "eyes wide shut" – and become easy prey for the murderous "crusaders" of Islam or their mouthpieces and defenders. Their purpose is the conquest of our minds – or their erasure.

https://edwardcline.blogspot.com/2015/12/eyes-wide-shut-political-correctness.html

Wednesday, February 10, 2016

Chapter 3: Huma Abedin: Wicked Witch of Islam

I sometimes have the fantasy of approaching Huma Abedin as a scout for Playboy Magazine and offering her a cover and foldout deal with the publication. I'm more curious about her possible response to such a proposition. Perhaps she would cast a voodoo hex on me, or a curse, or turn to a handy Muslim *djab* or imam to issue a fatwa. Or perhaps she'd just slap my face and sic the Secret Service goons on me. I've never seen her in a bathing suit, so I'm not sure about her figure. Perhaps she isn't Dallas Cheerleader material.

But she certainly is a fashion plate – unlike her boss, that aging Goodyear blimp in pantsuits – and apparently a well-paid one, at that. Huma is always expertly groomed, she looks like she lives comfortably in the nicest, safest neighborhoods, and possesses some poise, almost as much poise as Queen Noor of Jordan (Lisa Halaby) and that regal fox, Queen Rania, wife of King Abdullah.

But one would not be in error to claim that Huma Abedin is a card-carrying member of the Muslim Brotherhood. Or, shall we say, of the Muslim Sisterhood? Not so far-fetched a charge. There is an actual division of the Muslim Brotherhood called the Muslim Sisterhood. Hillary Clinton and Samantha Power are only honorary members of that organization, because they're not Muslims. But they, too, work against U.S. interests, and against

Israel's. They, too, wish to see Israel wiped from the map and the U.S. beholden to Islam.

.

There is so much dope on Huma Abedin that it could serve as raw material for a Mata Hari movie, and certainly enough to send her to prison at least on charges of treason, for helping Hillary breach national security, together with half a dozen other Federal felonies. She is, after all, an American citizen, born in 1976 in Kalamazoo, Michigan. There are several blog sites that contain all the necessary information that could be used to indict Abedin for at least acting as an agent against the U.S. for a foreign power, particularly Saudi Arabia, and generally, for the Muslim Brotherhood.

But, she's not a spy. Known spies are not usually invited to embed themselves in an enemy administration; and the Obama administration is definitely an enemy – of the U.S. Abedin fills the same role that Colonel House played to Woodrow Wilson, and that Harry Hopkins played to Franklin D. Roosevelt – a backseat position, mostly out of the limelight, but able to lean forward and whisper sweet-nothings of policy in the receptive executive's ear about what was practical and what wasn't. Abedin could also be compared to a high school driving instructor with his own steering wheel, and actually steer the ship of state in the right direction – "right" being whatever Islamic supremacists think is correct and proper and which conforms with the agenda established by the Muslim Brotherhood's and the Organization of Islamic Cooperation. For details on that alliance, see Stephen Coughlin's *Catastrophic Failure: The Blindfolding of America in the Face of Jihad.*

Huma Abedin is all for bringing into the U.S. as many Muslim "refugees" as possible. Which is tantamount to endorsing the introduction of Ebola and malaria into the national culture.

Discover the Networks has compiled a rap sheet on virtually every villain in American politics, and Huma Abedin has one of the longest dossiers. Her parental and political antecedents are not murky, but in plain view.

....Her father, Syed Abedin (1928-1993), was an Indian-born scholar who had worked as a visiting professor at Saudi Arabia's King Abdulaziz University in the early Seventies.

Huma's mother, Saleha Mahmood Abedin, is a sociologist known for her strong advocacy of Sharia Law. A member of the Muslim Sisterhood (i.e., the Muslim Brotherhood's division for women), Saleha is also a board member of the International Islamic Council for Dawa and Relief. This pro-Hamas entity is part of the Union of Good, which the U.S. government has formally designated as an international terrorist organization led by the Muslim Brotherhood luminary Yusuf al-Qaradawi.

The Center for Security Policy, in a special 2012 report on Abedin's mother, "Center Report Reveals Radical Islamist Views and Agenda of Senior State Department Official Huma Abedin's Mother," among other things lists the Sharia-compliant rules of living in Islamic society.

The Mother Bear, Saleha S.Mahmood Abedin

In light of the escalating controversy over the role being played in U.S. security policy-making by Ms. Abedin and others with personal and/or professional ties to the Muslim Brotherhood (see Part Eight of the Center for Security Policy's online curriculum at MuslimBrotherhoodinAmerica.com), the revelations contained in a new Center report— *Ties That Bind? The Views and Agenda of Huma Abedin's Islamist Mother*— could not be more timely, or important….

Excerpts from *Women in Islam* in *Ties That Bind? The Views and Agenda of Huma Abedin's Islamist Mother* include Islamic shariah justifications for the following practices (square brackets mine):

- Stoning for Adultery when Married; Lashing for Adultery when Unmarried [un-Islamic behavior will not be tolerated]
- No Death Penalty for the Murder of an Apostate [nor for the murder of an infidel]
- Freedom of Expression Curtailed to What Benefits Islam [censorship; no criticism by women or men of Islam; criticism of Islam doesn't much *benefit* it, does it?]
- Women's Right to Participate in Armed Jihad [knifing sprees in Israel, suicide vests, etc.]
- Social Interaction Between the Sexes is Forbidden [partitioned off from the men during prayers and even in Starbucks]
- Women Have No Right to Abstain from Sex with their Husbands [men cannot be denied their "rights"]
- A Woman Should Not Let Anyone Into the House Unless Approved by Her Husband [he wouldn't want any gays, Dallas Cheerleaders, or service dogs befouling his "castle"]
- Female Genital Mutilation is Allowed [to ensure that women experience no joy in sex]
- Man-Made Laws "Enslave Women" [didn't Allah say man-made laws are an abomination to him? Man-made laws also enslave Muslim men]

Daughter Huma has not repudiated any of this. At least, there is no report of her uttering a single word, pro or con, about her mother's endorsement of Fatima Umar Naseef's *Women in Islam: A Discourse on Rights and Obligations*, originally published in 1999 by International Islamic Committee for Woman & Child (IICWC).

President Barack Obama's February 3rd Baltimore mosque speech, says Steve Emerson of The Investigative Project on Terrorism, read like a Muslim Brotherhood script, a kind of long-winded pep talk to make Muslims feel good and cause everyone else hang their heads in shame. Who better to write such a speech than Huma Abedin? Her English language skills are impeccable, and beyond the range of Obama's composition skills.

A Muslim Sisterhood Movie Star, Huma Abedin, a career Clintonista

Discover the Networks traces Abedin's work life. She has not only been a career Clintonista, but an editor of an anti-West journal.

At age 18, Huma Abedin returned to the U.S. to attend George Washington University. In 1996 she began working as an intern in the Bill Clinton White House, where she was assigned to then-First Lady Hillary Rodham Clinton. Abedin was eventually hired as an aide to Mrs. Clinton and has worked for her ever since, through Clinton's successful Senate runs (in 2000 and 2006) and her failed presidential bid in 2008....

From 1996-2008, Abedin was employed by the Institute of Muslim Minority Affairs (IMMA) as the assistant editor of its in-house publication, the *Journal of Muslim Minority Affairs* (*JMMA*). At least the first seven of those years overlapped with the al Qaeda-affiliated Abdullah Omar Naseef's active presence at IMMA. Abedin's last six years at the Institute (2002-2008) were spent as a *JMMA* editorial board member; for one of those years, 2003, Naseef and Abedin served together on that board.

Throughout her years with IMMA, Abedin remained a close aide to Hillary Clinton. During Mrs. Clinton's 2008 presidential primary campaign, a *New York Observer* profile of Abedin described her as "a trusted advisor to Mrs. Clinton, especially on issues pertaining to the Middle East, according to a number of Clinton associates." "At meetings on the region," continued the profile, "... Ms. Abedin's perspective is always sought out."

And today Huma is "vice chair" of Hillary Clinton's imploding presidential campaign. Given Clinton's long and consistent record of bare-faced lying, hither-and-yon hiding, bilious blustering, and other crimes of her power-lusting hubris, "vice" is an appropriate name for the position.

It's all in the family, too, the Abedin *dawah* against the U.S. and the West. Aside from Saleha Abedin's literary excursions, as Discover the Networks concludes:

Huma Abedin's brother, Hassan Abedin, has ties to the Muslim Brotherhood and is currently an associate editor with the *JMMA*. Hassan was once a fellow at the Oxford Center for Islamic Studies, at a time when the Center's board included such Brotherhood-affiliated figures as Yusuf al-Qaradawi and Abdullah Omar Naseef.

Huma's sister, Heba Abedin (formerly known as "Heba A. Khaled"), is an assistant editor with *JMMA*, where she served alongside Huma prior to the latter's departure.

Huma Abedin is a witch, a wicked, conniving, embedded agent for Islam. Perhaps her laugh is more of a cackle, similar to that of the "Weird Ladies" in *Macbeth*. Or, better yet, like that of the Wicked Witch of the East. She's determined to get us, and our little dogs, too. We all know how Muslims are brought up to hate dogs and also cats. And pigs and Jews. And infidels. All stab-worthy.

https://edwardcline.blogspot.com/2016/02/huma-abedin-wicked-witch-of-islam.html

Saturday, December 26, 2015
Chapter 4: **The Islamic Candidate?**

Barack Obama as himself: The "Wolf" in the White House

I commented on a Daniel Greenfield FrontPage column of December 24th, "Muslim Immigration is Exactly What ISIS Wants." In it, Greenfield argues that ISIS wants to send thousands of its "fighters" to Europe and especially to the U.S., for the purpose of establishing operational bases for terrorism.

Agreeing with everything said by Mr. Greenfield concerning ISIS's tactics and overall strategy, a crucial question is: Because Obama wants to bring in tens of thousands of Muslim "refugees," and knows damned well there will be scores of ISIS agents among them, is this what he wants? Is he acting as an agent for ISIS? …I can posit an answer, but this is a question which would naturally occur to anyone observing Obama's actions and statements.

And that has been over the years, at least seven of them. In June 2008 I penned a five-part commentary on the rise of Barack Obama, "The Year of the Long Knives," which is accessible here. (That series does not mention Islam or Muslims even once. It dwells chiefly on the mooning crush on Obama our decrepit "aristocracy of money" has exhibited.) In this column I am positing an answer. It is purely speculative.

If it smacks of a "conspiracy theory," so be it. Because, after all, what exactly is a "conspiracy"? It is a plan, a long-range one, featuring many shadowy co-conspirators and their dupes and dogberries, together with secret funding and a knack for devious dissimulation. The term "conspiracy theory" has garnered the dubious distinction of being the exclusive preserve of garden variety kooks and of men who wear aluminum foil hats to better communicate with the aliens who are working with the Rosicrucians allied with the Elders of Zion to take over the earth.

And if there are observable, plausible, demonstrable dots to connect which, when connected, begin to show the outline and elements of a "conspiracy," then one has a "theory." Then the task is to pursue the devil in the details. Sometimes a conspiracy theory is structurally sound but empty of evidentiary details; other times there is, as Stephen Coughlin put it in *Catastrophic Failure*,

"...a tremendous amount of raw data. We denature it, break it into data bits, and pour it into a soft-science mold....The data on which our understanding is should have been based now serves only to buttress whichever theory is in vogue." (p. 453).

In short, the conspiracy theory may be rich in details but have no credible, realistic structure. It may be a thousand-piece jigsaw puzzle of blanks on which one can spray-paint any image but that of Islam.

However, there *is* a conspiracy afoot – one that has been walking the walk for many years – perhaps not even beginning with the Muslim Brotherhood's description in the 1991 Explanatory Memorandum of how to corrupt and take over America and the West, but even before that, say, in 1928 with the formation of the Muslim Brotherhood by Hassan al-Banna. Or in 1964 with the publication of *Milestones* by Sayyid Qutb, a Brotherhood member, whose advocacy of an incremental introduction of Sharia law is followed "religiously" by his successors.

In Obama's case, I do not think it is so much a conspiracy with

ISIS and Al-Qaeda, with the Muslim Brotherhood, with CAIR, with the ISNA, and with the Organization of Islamic Cooperation (OIC), as it is a simpatico, symmetrical, ideological marriage made in hell. Islam is totalitarian; and hates America. Obama's leftist ideology is totalitarian, and hates America. The alliance of the Left and Islam is a matter of record. Of course they would exploit each other's grand plan to bring down America. But I doubt very much there is buried email correspondence or communications between the White House and, say, Abu Bakr al-Baghdadi, the leader of the Islamic State, or anything like Hillary Clinton's surreptitious emails over Benghazi and her hidden bathroom email server.

So, I don't think Obama is our "Islamic Candidate," in the way of the half-witted character in 1962's *The Manchurian Candidate*. He was the garrulous, buffoonish husband, John Yerkes Iselin, played by James Gregory, of the power-lusting mistress of manipulation, played by Angela Lansbury (any resemblance in character between Mrs. Eleanor Shaw Iselin and Hillary Clinton is startlingly appropriate). She plotted to have his presidential running mate assassinated by her own son so her husband could take his place as the presidential candidate and very likely win the White House, where she would be the power in the Oval Office.

Obama, however, is not a half-wit; he knows what he's doing. He has stayed the course of his collectivist agenda ever since entering politics. He's shrewd, deceitful, glibly articulate, and a master of insouciance. That is my kinder description of him. But, is he Putin's poodle? Bill Clinton's gofer? Hillary Clinton's whipping boy? George Soros's puppet? Or Islam's useful idiot? Or is he just a "lone wolf" executive jihadi? I can't think of a single policy action of his, including the immigration issue, that hasn't if not immediately benefited the advance of Islam, later came home to roost.

So, is what ISIS wants, what Obama wants? Those reams of unintegrated data possibly presented to him in his morning security briefings – which Obama may or may not take seriously or even bother to read – must inform him of ISIS plans to infiltrate into the country with hordes of Syrian "refugees," and across the border from Mexico. If we, the public he wishes to deceive, are aware of these facts, can he not be, regardless of the accuracy and truth, or lack of such, in the information presented at his briefings? How can Obama *not* know what is going on?

I would say, yes, he knows. He has met with prominent Muslim figures overseas – who knows what was said between him and them behind closed doors? – when he met with Saudi kings and when he met with officials at Cairo University in 2009 and delivered his pro-Islam speech. His foreign policy agencies are top-heavy with "moderate" Muslims, all vetted with so-called security clearances. There are probably more Muslims in Obama's administration than there were Communists and fellow travelers in Roosevelt's. This cannot be as simple an issue of politically correct hiring policies – "we mustn't be beastly or discriminatory towards harmless American Muslims!" – but rather a signature characteristic of Obama's administration.

Greenfield's argument about how Muslim immigration benefits ISIS (and all the other implicated Islamic entities) is that the more Muslims are settled in Western countries, and especially in the U.S., the more potent their presence as colonizers and permanent "settlers" and as fifth-column type terrorists, ready to go into action once their jihadi psyche is triggered on orders from afar, or eclectically as individuals. Anything that enlarges the *Ummah*, or the global Islamic collective, benefits the Islamic Movement, even if it's only a small pocket of Somalis in Cheyenne, Wyoming. However, writes Greenfield:

The ritualistic "Why do they hate us" browbeating favored by the chattering classes is nonsense. Al Qaeda hated us because we were not Muslims. But it was only using us as the hated "other" to consolidate a collective Muslim identity. We are to Islamists what the Jews were to Hitler; a useful scapegoat whose otherness can be used to manufacture a contrasting pure Aryan or Islamic identity....

No dialogue is possible with an ideology whose virtue is premised on seeing you as utterly evil....

ISIS doesn't plan to defeat America through acts of terrorism. The plan for defeating America, like every other country, Muslim or non-Muslim, is to build a domestic Muslim terror movement that will be able to hold territory and swear allegiance to the Islamic State....

ISIS does not plan to defeat America with terror plots. But those plots will eventually accumulate into an organized domestic terror organization. An Islamic State in America based around a majority Muslim town or neighborhood with its own leader pledging allegiance to the Caliph of the Islamic State.

Dearborn, Michigan comes to mind. Greenfield:

Any Muslim plans for expanding into the West depend on Muslim immigration. Whether it's ISIS or its Muslim Brotherhood ancestor, or any of the other Islamist organizations and networks, they all require manpower. Some of that manpower will be provided by high Muslim birth rates, but it won't be nearly enough, not for a country the size of America, without a large annual flow of Muslim migrants.

We are told that halting Muslim immigration would only encourage Muslim terrorism. But our open door to Muslim immigration certainly hasn't stopped terrorism. Instead it has increased it by providing reinforcements to the terrorists. If we can't stop Muslim terrorism with the population we have now, how are we going to manage it if the Islamic population continues doubling and even tripling?

ISIS doesn't need to be "offended" by a call to halt Muslim immigration to the U.S. to launch terrorist attacks. It already has a plan, a doctrine, and an open conspiracy, as explained in that notorious *Explanatory Memorandum* from 1991:

"The process of settlement is a 'Civilization-Jihadist Process' with all the word means. The Ikhwan [Muslim Brotherhood] must understand that their work in America is a kind of grand jihad in eliminating and destroying the Western civilization from within and 'sabotaging' its miserable house by their hands and the hands of the believers so that it is eliminated and God's religion is made victorious over all other religions."

If Obama was ever Muslim Brotherhood friendly – and he certainly hailed the triumph of Mohamed Morsi and the Brotherhood in Egypt, and even, with Hillary Clinton, contributed to Morsi's rise, albeit it lasted only a year – he had to have had knowledge of the *Explanatory Memorandum*. He has to know that the Brotherhood's overall doctrine, which is identical to ISIS's, and CAIR's, and the OIC's, is to impose Sharia on the West and most particularly on the U.S.

Further on ISIS's preference for an enabled immigration of Muslims, Greenfield notes:

Even if we defeat ISIS tomorrow, Al Qaeda and other Islamist groups descended from the Muslim Brotherhood will continue pursuing the same goals. And they will rely on the Muslim population in the United States to provide them with money, supplies, cover and an infrastructure for terrorism.

ISIS can't defeat us with terror attacks. The only hope for an enduring Islamic victory over America is through the rise of domestic groups that pledge allegiance to the Caliphate. ISIS can't invade America. It has to be invited in. That's what our immigration policy does. Trump isn't a threat to national security. Muslim immigration is....

Muslim immigration is the Islamic State's only hope for victory over America.

In terms of imposing Sharia law on the U.S., it is also the hope of the Muslim Brotherhood, the OIC, and CAIR, among all the other Islamic front groups now in the country.

Earlier, I mentioned George Soros. No conspiracy theories need be fashioned where he is concerned. He has openly supported Obama's program to "transform" the country and has meddled in no little way to steer U.S. foreign policy to his liking, which has been the diminution of American influence and the reduction of the country into a Balkanized collection of warring pressure, religious, and ethnic groups. His "rap sheet" on Discover the Networks is several pages long. Obama was certainly Soros's preferred candidate. This is described in New York Magazine's October 2007 article, "Money Chooses Sides."

The investment banker Robert Wolf first met Barack Obama one afternoon in December in a midtown conference room. Obama was in town to deliver a speech at a charity dinner for children in poverty at the Mandarin Oriental—but also to pursue another, less high-minded, but more momentous, objective: to begin the process of attempting to pick Hillary Clinton's pocket.

The conference room belonged to George Soros, the billionaire bête noire of the right. After talking to Soros for an hour about his prospective bid for the White House, Obama walked down the hall and found assembled a dozen of the city's heaviest-hitting Democratic fund-raisers: investment banker Hassan Nemazee, Wall Street power Blair Effron, private-equity hotshot Mark Gallogly, hedge-fund manager Orin Kramer. Most had been big-time John Kerry backers in 2004. Most had a connection to the Clintons. All were officially uncommitted for 2008.

I have no idea why the author of the article, John Heilemann, would characterize Soros as "the billionaire bête noire of the right," when Soros is of the global government left. But then journalists from the left usually see any billionaire as a right-wing, knuckle-dragging fascist. And Heilemann has a master's

degree from the <u>John F. Kennedy School</u> of Government at
Harvard, which can explain his confusion. Further, it is
billionaires like Soros, Bill Gates, Warren Buffet, Mark
Zuckerberg, and others who have become the voluble vanguard
of global socialism.

The Messiah cometh to his adoring flock of wealthy children. New
York Magazine, October 2007: Obama speaking at a fund-raiser at
Steven and Judy Gluckstern's home, April 9, 2007. George Soros, in a
blue shirt, is seated to the left of Obama, looking bored but smugly
satisfied with what he is hearing.

Is Soros a conspirator? I think so. In his role as a spread-the-
wealth,   Yes-you-built-that-but-we're-going-to-take-it-anyway
gadfly, he has spoken against national borders. This was revealed
in a November Breitbart article, "<u>Soros Admits Involvement in
Migrant Crisis</u>." In response to Hungarian Prime Minister Viktor
Orban's accusation that Soros was one of the movers behind the
hordes of migrants crossing European borders, Soros sent an
email:

Mr. Soros has now issued an <u>email</u> statement to *Bloomberg
Business*, claiming his foundations help "uphold European
values", while Mr. Oban's actions in strengthening the
Hungarian border and stopping a huge migrant influx
"undermine those values."

"His plan treats the protection of national borders as the
objective and the refugees as an obstacle," Mr. Soros added.
"Our plan treats the protection of refugees as the objective and
national borders as the obstacle."

Yes, national borders are obstacles. Aside from helping define the character of a nation, they also serve the same purpose as fences, doors, windows, and locks, which help to frustrate trespassers, burglars, home invaders, and other predators. It is a nation's identity that Soros wants to erase.

In 2006, FrontPage interviewed Richard Poe, the co-author of *The Shadow Party: How George Soros, Hillary Clinton, and Sixties Radicals Seized Control of the Democratic Party.* Among other things, Poe said:

The Shadow Party is always changing. New groups form and old ones dissolve. For instance, America Coming Together -- which raised $135 million for Democrat get-out-the-vote drives in 2004 – has been mothballed, at least for now. The most active Shadow Party groups today are probably the Center for American Progress, America Votes, Democracy Alliance, the New Democrat Network, the New Politics Institute, ACORN and, of course, MoveOn.org.

In his new book *The Age of Fallibility*, Soros writes, "*The main obstacle to a stable and just world order is the United States.*" He announced in 2003 that it is necessary to "puncture the bubble of American supremacy." Soros is working systematically to achieve that goal. (*Italics* mine)

So is Obama. Is this why Soros backed Obama's run for the presidency? He certainly placed the right bet. But did Soros also see Obama as an ideal Islamic Candidate as long ago as 2007? Doubtless. Soros's role in the mass invasion of Europe didn't show until there was resistance to his "open society/open borders" notion began to manifest itself, especially in Eastern Europe.

As Pamela Geller reports in her October Atlas Shrugs article, "World Leader SLAMS George Soros for promoting, funding 'migrant' invasion":

His tentacles are everywhere. Muslim migrants arriving in Europe are given a 'migrants handbook' packed with tips, maps, phone numbers and advice about getting across Europe. The "rough guide" contains phone numbers of organizations which might help refugees. The 'rough guide' is written in Arabic and contains phone numbers of organizations which will help refugees making the journey, such as the Red Cross and UNHCR. The "Rough Guide", being printed and distributed by the Soros "Open Society" group "W2eu" or "Welcome to the EU", Foundations, has activists handing out these guides for free in Turkey.

And how can one account for all the cell phones, tennis shoes, clothing, backpacks, and other personal items carried by the thousands of healthy male "refugees" posing as impoverished Syrians fleeing the chaos of the Syrian civil war, or from Libya, Somalia, and the Balkans? Too likely these were also distributed free by Soros through Open Society or some other NGO he controls.

In conclusion, I would mark Barack Obama as every Islamic collectivist's perfect candidate to help advance Islam in the West and around the world. That may or may not be Soros's religious cup of tea, but I don't think it would make any difference to him who or what dissolves the West in the name of whatever fantasy world he imagines the world ought to be. That is the nature of the poisonous, maleficent ball of glop that is Soros's "soul," which only a Fyodor Dostoyevsky would have the fortitude to examine in depth.

And, because so much of Obama's past is either closed to scrutiny (e.g., his not releasing much information about his academic career) or off limits to any kind of "shovel-ready" investigating reporting.

Only Obama knows for sure whether or not he is "The Islamic Candidate." And his actions, speeches, and policies over the last seven years are certainly not calculated to discourage the idea.

https://edwardcline.blogspot.com/2015/12/the-islamic-candidate.html

Saturday, January 2, 2016

Chapter 5: Interfaith Bridges to Islam

Writing as an atheist, I at first thought it would be difficult to comment on a specific part of Stephen Coughlin's *Catastrophic Failure: Blindfolding America in the Face of Jihad*, which is Part XI: Interfaith Outreach (Appendix One, pp. 511-574). But Coughlin presents the subject in such clear terms that it was fascinating and definitely instructive to observe how the Islamic Movement ensnares Christians and Jews in "interfaith dialogue" for the Muslim Brotherhood's own nefarious purposes. Much of the slithering methods of the interfaith dialogue promoted by various Islamic organizations, which can be viewed as a master template, can be seen in how Muslim "experts" in Islam are used to help American counter-intelligence formulate useless and vacuous analyses of threats by ISIS and al-Qaeda and other terrorist groups, which is also exhaustively detailed by Coughlin in his book.

Readers and fans of my novels know that I can mock any religion, but refrain from such business in real life because all those religions but one are not out of kill, convert, or subjugate me. They leave me alone, I leave them alone. Except for Mormon and Jehovah Witnesses door-knockers, who are mostly unsolicited pests. They're not on my doorstep for long.

The exception is Islam.

The biggest beneficiary of postmodernism – that is, the broad movement of denial of the value and efficacy of reason – aside from the Democrats, aside from the "trigger warning" and "safe place" addicts, aside from the advocates of open borders, aside from the advocates of moral relativism, aside from gun-control advocates, aside from Black Lives Matter, aside from the assailants on the First Amendment, and etc., is Islam. In the suffocating, mind-stunting miasma of postmodernist thought and practice in Western culture, the biggest victor is and will continue to be Islam.

Postmodernism has allowed Islam unopposed and unparalleled entrée into the minds and values of Westerners. Coughlin discusses how this entrée works and the consequences of Christian and Jewish religionists compromising their own beliefs by agreeing to form a "united front" for peace and coexistence and multi-beliefs with Islam. He correctly identifies the chief culprit and enabler of Muslim Brotherhood-dominated interfaith dialogue as postmodernism. Postmodernism is not incidental to the inroads being made by Islam in the West. It is a key factor.

Without the assist of postmodernism – which Islam did not create – neither the Brotherhood nor the Organization of Islamic Cooperation (OIC) could exploit the self-criticism of the West nor inveigle their way into the language and behavior of non-Muslim interfaith participants. Islam would be stopped cold, told to return to the miserable pestholes from which it came, and not admitted through the gates of Aristotelian thought. The shiny shield of reason consistently applied to everything and every idea, could not be breached by the underhanded finagling and deft finessing machinations of the Brotherhood and the OIC.

A West that doubts or questions its own value qua West is destined for destruction, either by Islam or by "its own hands."

Islam will provide the rope.

Islam has proved adept in exploiting the anti-reason, anti-man culture of the postmodern world. But its somersaults and linguistic gymnastics would fall flat in a one hundred percent Aristotelian West.

What is postmodernism? Britannica Online has a succinct description:

Postmodernism as a philosophical movement is largely a reaction against the philosophical assumptions and values of the modern period of Western (specifically European) history—i.e., the period from about the time of the scientific revolution of the 16th and 17th centuries to the mid-20th century. Indeed, many of the doctrines characteristically associated with postmodernism can fairly be described as the straightforward denial of general philosophical viewpoints that were taken for granted during the 18th-century Enlightenment, though they were not unique to that period.

For example:

The descriptive and explanatory statements of scientists and historians can, in principle, be objectively true or false. The postmodern denial of this viewpoint—which follows from the rejection of an objective natural reality—is sometimes expressed by saying that there is no such thing as Truth.

The Brotherhood and the OIC would agree: There is no such thing as Truth – except for the "truth" of Islam. And what is it that the Brotherhood and the OIC have had successes in corrupting, sabotaging, and misdirecting?

Reason and logic are universally valid—i.e., their laws are the same for, or apply equally to, any thinker and any domain of knowledge. For postmodernists, reason and logic too are merely conceptual constructs and are therefore valid only within the established intellectual traditions in which they are used.

Coughlin begins "Interfaith Outreach" with:

While penetrating government and civil organizations is important, the interfaith movement constitutes a major supporting line of operations in Brotherhood penetration operations. Through subversion of the interfaith community, the Brotherhood seeks to manipulate other religions in furtherance of dislocating their faith. [Its ultimate goal being the imposition of Sharia law.] Regarding the interfaith community, the "hands of the believers" are primarily the Brotherhood and Islamic Movement participants, while "their hands" refers to those non-Muslim clerics (ministers, priests, and rabbis) who help facilitate the mission of "eliminating and destroying Western civilization from within." [Excerpted from the Brotherhood _Explanatory Memorandum_ of 1991.] Because a Quranic basis exists for what the Brotherhood strategy states is its intent,   all interfaith activities emanating from or involving known Brotherhood groups should be viewed with this understanding. (p. 512)

Imams and other Muslims who meet with non-Muslim clerics are not so much having a "dialogue" as engaging in _dawah_, or Islamic proselytizing. It is a one-way street, and the non-hostile, non-threatening conviviality of Muslim clerics with the clerics of the People of the Book (Christians and Jews, called in the _Koran_ apes and pigs) blinds the clerics to what is actually happening.

Coughlin discusses at length book published in 2011 by the International Institute for Islamic Thought (IIIT), based in Herndon, Virginia., _Interfaith Dialogue: A Guide for Muslims_, by Muhammad Shatfiq and Mohammed Abu-Nimmer. It is a kind of guide of what to do and say and what not to or say when having a "dialogue" with non-Muslim clerics.

From another Islamic publication, _The Methodology of Dawah Illallah in American Perspective,_ by Shamin Siddiqi, published in 1989 by The Forum for Islamic Work, based in Brooklyn,

New York, Coughlin quotes from Siddiqi on the similarities between that publication and *Interfaith Dialogue*:

The I.M.O.A. [Islamic Movement in America – an early designation for the Muslim Brotherhood in America] will open dialogues with dignitaries of the religious institutions, presenting Islam as the common legacy of Judeo-Christian religions and as the only Guidance now available to mankind in its most perfect form for its *Falah* (Deliverance and Salvation). These talks must be held in a **very friendly and non-aggressive atmosphere**, as directed by Allah (SWT) in the Qur'an as to how to talk with people of the scripture – *"And argue not with the people of the Scripture unless it be in a way that is better."* [bold the author's] (Al- Qur'an -- 28,.46)

The "common legacy," Muslim dialogue participants will not enlighten their opposite numbers with, is that the Koran historically was a work-in-progress over centuries that cadged from Judeo-Christian texts and lore. Coughlin:

As Siddiqi stated, the Brotherhood views the methodologies used in dawah as prescribed by Allah. When assessing the intentions of the Brotherhood's work product, it is important to remember that is manner of communication is generally consistent with Omar Ahmad's requirements to send two messages in the same communication:

…We will recognize the source of any message which comes out of us…if a message is publicized, we will know…the media person among us will recognize that you send two messages; **one to the Americans and one to the Muslims….** (Bold Coughlin's]

Coughlin highlights what non-Muslim clerics ought to know about the Brotherhood's ends that is rooted in Sayyid Qutb's *Milestones,* but don't know because they are too enthralled by the prospect of having a dialogue with Muslims without being cursed out or killed.

Another indicator that *interfaith Dialogue* reflects the Muslim Brotherhood mission is the repeated allusion to bridge building. Sayyid Qutb used this term in *Milestones* to set the limits of dawah interaction with non-Muslims: "the chasm between Islam and *Jahiliyyah* [society and government of unbelievers, or, pagan ignorance; specifically, a pre-Koranic state of ignorance]is great, and a bridge is not to be built across it so that the people on the two sides may mix with each other, but only so that the people of Jahiliyyah may come over to Islam." P. 515)

In short, the interfaith dialogue "bridge" only exists, as far as the Muslim Brotherhood is concerned, to facilitate non-believers to cross over to Islam. It's a one-way bridge. Muslims will never cross it to join the non-believers.

There's more. Why are Muslim clerics so eager to share the same air with infidel clerics? Coughlin writes:
Interfaith Dialogue positions <u>*Hudaybiyah*</u> [a ten-year "treaty," actually a truce, between Mohammad and Meccans in 628 A.D.] to establish the claim the Prophet had an overwhelming interest in maintaining peace, even going so far as entering into treaties that were unpopular and humiliating. *Interfaith Dialogue* states:

The treaty shows that the Prophet preferred peace even at the cost of annoying some of his close followers. He knew that peaceful living would allow Muslims to dialogue with non-Muslims, move about freely, and build relations with other tribes. The treaty is an excellent example of giving the extra mile with others to achieve peace.

But, there's a catch, which Coughlin details.

Without an awareness of Islamic law [Sharia], interfaith partners read this observation and think it reflects an ongoing commitment to peace grounded in an explicit preference of the Prophet. Yet a quick reference to *Reliance of the Traveller* makes it clear that this is not the case. The relevant shariah is in the section on jihad concerning truces. *Reliance* shows that Islamic law does not permit treaties, but recognizes only truces that are made on a short-term basis. Of note, *Interfaith Dialogue* erroneously designates *Hudaybiyyah*as a treaty, not a truce.

Further, because truces require the nonperformance of jihad, truces are disfavored, cannot be entered into merely to preserve the status quo, and can only be made in times when Muslim weakness, lack of numbers, or because the other side may convert to Islam. (p. 516)

Briefly, no member of the tripartite alliance of *jihad, dawah, and ummah* in the organizing principle, which is Sharia, can nullify, frustrate, or contradict the other two. They work together as one entity in an aggressive ideological *gestalt*.

Non-Muslim interfaith partners are misled or deluded when they encounter in their "dialogue" with their Muslim opposite numbers such terms as "peace," "goodwill," "justice," "injustice," "liberty of thought," and "human rights." They do not realize, or do not care to know, that these terms only apply to Muslims. "Peace" is the peace of a global caliphate. "Goodwill" is extended solely to Muslims. "Justice and "injustice" apply only to Muslims. "Liberty of thought" means being "free" to convert to Islam. And only Muslims have "human rights." Non-

Muslims are "tolerated" only if they pay the *jizya* or poll tax imposed by Islamic authorities. If they refuse, they die.

When Christian and Jewish clerics read something like:

Islam is not an arbitrary religion, nor has it ever ordered Muslims to force others to adopt it even though it is the final and complete revelation from God. He says: "Let there by no compulsion in religion. Truth stands out clear from error." (Sayyid Qutb, in *Islam and Universal Peace*, Q.II.256). (pp. 518-519)

...their "hearts and minds" go aflutter at the prospect of "getting along" with their Muslim "brothers," unaware that the words they are familiar with mean that it is an issue of converting to Islam. The phrase, "Let there be no compulsion in religion" is an invitation to *voluntarily* convert to Islam, that the "Truth" is Islam, and that the "error" is their Christianity or Jewish faith.

Coughlin notes:

> When Jewish or Christian "partners" work with Muslim Brothers who declare a complete commitment to peace, are they aware of what is being committed to? The only thing worse than interfaith partners not knowing the Brotherhood's agenda when they engage in outreach with them is that some partners *may* know. As shepherds of their respective flocks, interfaith leaders should take the time to know the equities and interests of all parties. Shepherds who cannot recognize the wolf are not good shepherds. (p. 519)

When meeting with their Muslim interfaith partners, there are rules that govern the "give and take" about what to say about one's religion. But, with Islam, it's all "take" and very little "give." It's the Jews and Christians who must do the "soul searching" and "reflection" about the "truth" of their faiths. The terms "reciprocity," "trust," and "honesty" might be in the dialogue lexicon, but they're not observed by the Muslims. "Reciprocity," in the context of interfaith dialogue, for Muslims is nearly akin to *shirk* or apostasy, while "honesty" about Islam is right out. The truth about Islam might frighten the "partners" away, and that would be the end of the dialogue. The Brotherhood has invested too much effort in getting the infidel clerics to "sabotage their miserable faiths by their own hands" and at the hands of the Brotherhood to indulge in frank and brutal honesty about Islam and their goals. "Trust," to Muslims, is an understanding that their interfaith "partners" will not ask Muslims embarrassing questions that would require Muslims to bare their true intentions. Not that they ever would in any circumstance.

But Christian and Jewish dialogue partners are so anxious to "iron things out "with their Muslim opposite numbers that they are virtually hypnotized by their own delusions about what is possible. In effect, they become subordinate to the Muslim clerics, because the dialogue is conducted solely on Islamic terms. This is in keeping with the Islamic goal of becoming the dominant religion; no concessions are made by Muslim interfaith partners. The "bridge" they throw across the chasm of doctrinal differences is meant for the infidel clerics to cross over to Islam. Muslims will never set foot on it.

There are, writes Coughlin, Jewish and Christian clerics who know what the score is, yet continue the interfaith dialogue charade and have prestige invested in it. They are willing to compromise – and even betray – their core religious beliefs to publically meet their Muslim opposite numbers "half way," knowing that their Muslim "partners" are in the game for the whole pot. Coughlin writes:

Interfaith rules are thinly veiled postmodern assaults on reason that succeed by undermining basic principles of logic. (p. 523)

Coughlin cites the three laws of Aristotelian logic – the law of identity, the law of the non-contradiction, and the law of the excluded middle – to drive home his point that Jewish and Christian clerics, visi-a-vis their religious principles, are products of our postmodern culture. They are willing to accept the contradictions, and hang all their hopes and wishes for a multifaith *détente* on a phantom excluded middle. They are fascinated with and entranced by the crocodile that smiles at them, unaware that sooner or later, the crocodile will attack and eat them, but not before drowning them in their own folly.

Catastrophic Failure: Blindfolding America in the Face of Jihad, by Stephen Coughlin. Washington DC: Center for Security Policy Press, 2015. 788 pp.

https://edwardcline.blogspot.com/2016/01/interfaith-bridges-to-islam.html

Friday, September 9, 2016

Chapter 6: A Halloween Special

They'll come knocking on your door soon in various costumes, some of them downright scary. They're not kiddies, but full grown adults, and if you don't give them what they want, they'll do worse than soap your door or lather your car in shaving cream or "key" your car's finish. They have much, much worse in mind. They'll seize your house, or burn it down with you in it.

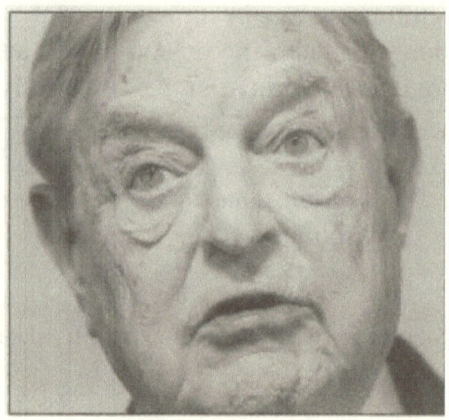

George Soros
A Halloween mask that might be found at Wal-Mart

You all recognize his decaying, decrepit visage, don't you? It's the kind of face you'd encounter if you opened a coffin after it had been sitting in the sun for two or three days. Or for a week. Of course, it's George Soros, the man(?) who wants to see Israel reduced to ashes and overrun by Palestinian Muslim savages, America reduced to the status of Sweden, France, and Germany (also overrun by Muslim savages), America's white population whipped into chattel slavery, the global economy run by his statist, mercantilist rules, who has proposed that the Internet be closed to anyone who questions his Marxist agenda for an "open society", a man[?] whose "best years" of his life were when he was helping the Nazis steal other Hungarian Jews' property, who wants to remake the world in his own "Dorian Gray" image. He is a creature whose blood must not be red, but rather greenish black bile.

"If truth be known, I carried some rather potent messianic fantasies with me from childhood," fantasies which "I wanted to indulge ... to the extent that I could afford. (George Soros, *Underwriting Democracy*, p. 3)

Soros today recalls the German occupation of Hungary as "probably the happiest years of my life." (Michael Lewis, "The Speculator," *New Republic* (January 10-17, 1994)

"I realized [as a young man] that it's money that makes the world go round," says Soros, "so I might as well make money.... But having made it, I could then indulge my social concerns." Invariably, those concerns center around a desire to change the world generally—and America particularly—into something new, something consistent with his vision of "social justice." (Faisal Islam, "Rich Man, Wise Man" (*Observer*: March 10, 2002)

This man(?) holds such a depth of malice for America and the West that he'd rather see them destroyed, and he has poured most of his ill-gotten gains into ensuring that this comes about. His "Open Society" Foundation is surely a glaring misnomer, for it advocates anything but an "open society," but rather a society closed to individualism, national sovereignty, and *laissez faire*. About Soros's Open Society Foundation

The term "open society" had been originally coined in 1932 by the French philosopher Henri Louis Bergson, to describe societies whose moral codes were founded upon "universal" principles seeking to enhance the welfare of all mankind—as opposed to "closed" societies that placed self-interest above any concern for other nations and cultures. [Philosopher Karl] Popper readily embraced this concept and expanded upon it. In his view, the open society was a place that permitted its citizens the right to criticize and change its institutions as they saw fit; he rejected the imposed intellectual conformity, central planning, and historical determinism of Marxist doctrine.

Soros's "open society," however, in all its manifestations, would be a suffocating straightjacket of intellectual conformity (political correctness), central planning (Soviet or Nazi or Obama style), and the government-mob organized hounding of anyone who criticized or threatened the statist status quo. (See the vitriolic opposition to Donald Trump's presidential candidacy by the intellectual class, the MSM, and the #NeverTrump Republicans, for a taste of how "open" that kind of society can be.)

Soon she will be as ugly as her America-hating mother.

Huma Abedin is The Muslim Brotherhood's "inside man" in American government and especially in Hillary Clinton's career in Washington. What would Huma Abedin look like without undergoing a total Vanity Fair make-over and being subjected to all of Hollywood's cosmetic special effects arts to make her presentable to the public? Nothing, I think, you would want to wake up next to in the morning. Unless you were Hillary Clinton. Hillary's "confidante" and political gadfly has been a permanent presence in the Clinton claque for years. She has no security clearance whatsoever, it having been waived at the insistence of Clinton. See my article, "Huma Abedin" on Rule of Reason from February 2016, "Huma Abedin: Wicked Witch of Islam."

Would like to be appointed to the Supreme Court

Barack Obama needs no introduction here. His record of destruction of this country is "legend." Shall we name the ways: ObamaCare, unrestricted immigration of the cultural and political enemies of this country to bolster the Democrats, a refusal to credit Islam for the horrendous terrorist attacks world-wide and in this country, the destruction of our military, the destruction of the coal industry, his numerous crony capitalist scandals and failure, and on and on. Quite a "legacy" of sticking it to the country in the name of Saul Alinsky.

Cackle, Cackle! Cough! Cough!

There is Hillary Clinton, another wicked witch, another protégé of Alinsky, who promises to complete the nihilist work begun by Obama. She can't wait to get her hands on the country. Among her first priorities as "president" will be the shutting down or shackling of the Internet and anyone in it who objects to her policies which would also complement her dedication to Sharia law. She hosted an OIC conference. This comports well with the Soros proposal to close the Internet to all but supporters of the "closed society."

There's James Carville, a career Democratic advisor, commentators, and strategist who helped the Clintons and Obama win office, and many of the worst dictators on the planet. He strikes many people as an iconic villain of the worst fright films.

Let us now turn to a bigger band of Halloween tricksters-and-treaters: the MSM. While the new thug/killer of The Walking Dead, Negan, has become the preferred *bête noire* of the series, that's more a reflection on The Walking Dead's loopy fan base, many of which would prefer to see evil in the driver's seat over a band of heroes.

I think I've figured out why the MSM is smitten with Hillary; it's the same reason why Negan's minions obey without question.

Hillary's alter ego: Negan of *The Walking Dead*

him, although he's armed with only a baseball bat and most of his followers are armed with automatic weapons any one of which could cut him to pieces., no one dares oppose him. *It's because they like it that way, they can live with subservience.* Freedom is an anathema to them. They'd rather be told what to do, and why, they'd rather be psychologically and physically subservient to a head-bashing tyrant, even though their real-life doppelgangers have full knowledge of Hillary's crimes, misdemeanors and treason. They're comfortable with it. Turning Negan away from your door and not giving him any candy (which he's already claimed is not yours anymore, can earn you an instant head-bashing with his baseball bat, questioning the ends and means and character of Hillary Clinton will earn you a similar fate: the end of your career, your financial ruin, banishment from journalism, perhaps even an untimely death (there have been precedents of the latter punishment).

Kowtowing to Negan has the same mental roots as kowtowing to Hillary.

They're comfortable in the proximity of evil

Take a look at this photo of the U.S. press adoring Hillary on her new campaign plane. Is this not frightening? These are not only adults, but alleged "journalists." Do not these bobble heads fit the psychological profile of cultists? Are they not in ecstatic thrall to the very symbol of evil? The apotheosis of evil and unmitigated corruption – because they "work," because evil seems to have more "efficacy" than good? Are they not on the same level as Negan's hundreds of gun-toting slaves? Perhaps it's the prospect of being a new "insider" or being appointed to Hillary's cabinet.

You really want to know what drives anyone to sell his self-respect. As The Walking Dead's fan base let its fascination and obsessions be known to the producers – who have tailored the new Seasons to these scary preferences – the MSM has let its preferences be known. Hillary's and her husband's crimes roll off their psyches like water off of a duck. They're comfortable with it all; it saves them the trouble of moral judgement and the necessity of having the least fealty to truth and reality.

"To hell with Hillary's crimes," they all chortle. "We want to help make the world as she envisions it. It's not right to pass moral judgments on her."

Happy Halloween!

https://edwardcline.blogspot.com/2016/09/a-halloween-special.html

Tuesday, February 2, 2016

Chapter 7: Sergeant Schultz Knows Everything

"I know *nothing!*"

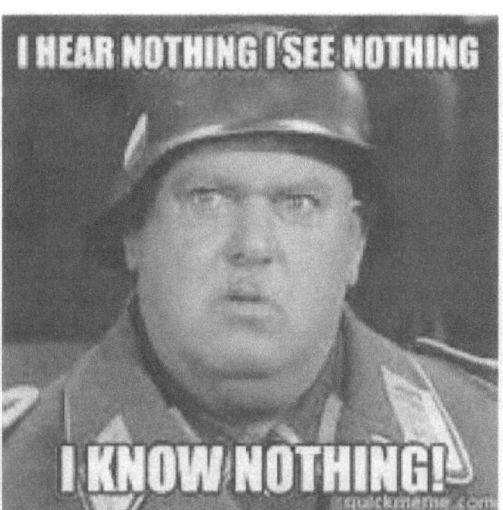

He was really a totalitarian, but a soft-hearted
one. He'd impose a modest fine or let you live the
balance of your life in prison for having offended
or harmed a Muslim in self-defense.

That was Sergeant Hans Schultz's favorite and well-known
refrain in *Hogan's Heroes,* which ran on CBS from 1965 to
1971. In the linked clip, he adds, "I was not here! I did not even
get up this morning!"

Suppose you had a chance to chat with the real-life Sgt. Schultz's
in Germany, Sweden, Norway, Denmark. The "interfaith"
dialogue would go something like this, after you've reported a
crime committed by a Muslim.

Sgt. Schultz will claim that he knows everything, he was there,
and that you should go back to sleep and pretend nothing ever
happened. You were not raped by a Muslim or a gang of
Muslims. You did not have your head kicked in by a gang of
Muslims. You were not robbed by a Muslim. Or stabbed, or

groped, or spit on by a Muslim on a train or on the street. Or even raped and then disfigured by a Muslim. Or by a "refugee," or by an "immigrant."

All right, Sgt. Schultz would concede. All or one of those things happened to you. There's no denying the facts, is there? But if you fought back, and used illegal means such as pepper spray to deter your assailant, then you must be punished. Your fighting back is evidence of bigotry, or racism, of being anti-Muslim or anti-Islam or anti-immigrant. Of your lack of patriotism! Those states of mind are illegal, as well, and must be corrected.

You must allow yourself to be raped, robbed, and spit on. It's your duty to submit to the diktats of Islam. You must submit to Sharia. Horridly primitive system, yes. But, who are we to judge? You may not survive the experience, but it's an issue of sacrifice. Of self-sacrifice for the greater good. For the nation. Sweden, Denmark, Norway, Finland, Germany, even Italy – all of our lily-white societies, have a duty to be invaded and assaulted by Muslims and others. We have a duty to relieve the suffering they endured in the countries from which they came. We have no right to assert that our morals and our society are superior to the cultures of the immigrants. We have no right to impose them on immigrants, even here. That is the height of cultural hubris and civilizational imperialism. Okay, so the perpetrator was Somalian. And he hates whites, even though Sweden was not a party to the downfall of Somalia. Or Ethiopia. I'm a little foggy on the history of that part of the world. So what?

Don't you understand that when a black- or brown- or olive-skinned male immigrant rapes a Swede or a German, it's what the Americans would call "payback" for the destruction and looting of the immigrant's home country? And even if the destruction and looting are purely imaginary, and you or your ancestors had nothing to do with it, you're still guilty. The purpose is to humiliate and degrade the victim, to demonstrate who's in charge now. You may call it racism on his part; but from his perspective, it's reparations. Sure, it's racism. But it's justifiable racism. Also, It's a religious requirement to rape non-Muslim women, and beat up non-Muslim men within an inch of their lives. I suspect that's just an excuse for a super-excited Muslim to get his jollies off, but don't tell anyone I said that.

You say you have a right to know what's going on in the country, about all the crimes committed by Muslims and other immigrants? *Gott im Himmel*! How naïve of you! No, you don't have a right to know! Nobody not in government or the police forces has a right to know! If people knew, there'd be a furious backlash at immigrants, and Muslims, they might be attacked, and hurt, or even killed!

But you say *they* have a right to attack, hurt, and even kill native Swedes, and Danes, and Germans, without much consequence, just a slap on the wrist? But, that's their culture, and we can't punish them for acting out their culture! That would be...discriminatory! And that's unthinkable! We don't want to be charged with racism, or religious bigotry, or anti-Muslimism! God, if we reported every one of the 5,000 or more crimes committed by Muslims, we'd have to deport the whole lot of them! Or jail them. The newspapers would run out of space to report them all! But, they've saved themselves the trouble of being disciplined for reporting news we don't want reported. They don't want to start a panic, either!

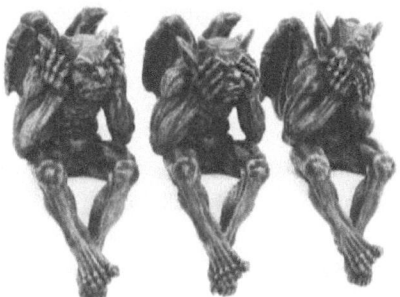

Hear no evil, see no evil, speak no evil. Government and media gargoyles at work, and Facebook, too.

There's a fellow in America who ought to be silenced, Daniel Greenfield, he helped to spill the beans on our secret Code 291 policy, which is to secretly compiled statistics on Muslim and immigrant crimes committed in Sweden but not report them to the public. He wrote such slanderous things about our law-enforcement efforts. He made much of that silly goose, Alexandra Mezher, who got herself killed trying to break up a fight between "asylum seekers children." Poor girl, but that's the risk you take when you do the right thing and help adult children settle into our lovely country. I feel no remorse for her. Sooner or later she was going to be sexually assaulted, but that's neither here nor there. So it's good she's dead. But this Greenfield fellow, he wrote – and don't you go broadcasting this to anyone else, not even to your parents, or else you can be charged with hate speech and that carries a heavier penalty than using illegal pepper spray, or Mace:

The people at the top wanted an overview of the crisis, but they did not want the public to know what was going on. That was what Code 291 was for....

Police would not disclose details of the resources spent on work with refugees and migrants. This despite the fact that the agency kept separate statistics on this using the secret code "291" .

This is not how democracies work. This is not how free countries work. This is how totalitarian states work.

European governments are deliberately hiding information about Muslim migrant crimes from the public. They are covering up attacks, intimidating witnesses and even visiting the homes of people who criticize this on Twitter to intimidate them.

This is what a totalitarian system looks like. Code 291 should be a rallying call to bring down the iron curtain of collectivist bureaucracy and expose the truth about its migrant hordes.

What libelous, xenophobic rubbish! We are not *totalitarian*! What a nasty slur! We are a caring regime. Sometimes we overdo it, but it's all for your own good. It's all for the general good. You can't create a model society of diversity and multiculturalism without breaking a few traditions or taboos or heads.

Are you saying that the Swedish and German and Danish police have become *allies* of the criminals?? That suggestive libel has earned you extra two years in the clink! So what if the Cologne police have erased all visual record of the mass assault on women there on New Year's Eve? It's for the public's own good. That great prophetess Chancellor Angela Merkel, is determined to make Germans and Germany pay for its past crimes, even though most Germans alive today had nothing to do with Nazism, they weren't even born yet!

Still, it's the cultural and political heritage thing, you know, and their inherited "white privilege" that must be paid for. And so what if no Somali or Iraqi or Turk or Syrian never discovered a new law of physics or invented new medical procedure (other than beheading!) or composed anything worth listening to. They come from brutal societies with their own cultural heritage. We mustn't be judgmental now. Or else you spend a night in the box! Love that American phrase! But that Greenfield writer is definitely *not* to my taste!

Our dear friend Mr. Mark Zuckerberg ought to shut him up! Hate speech just causes problems. Hate is contagious, you know, especially if the object of hate is, well...hateful. And you can hate all of these immigrants, but also feel sorry for them.

Now, if you can't pay the 5,000 Euro fine, you'll have to be cuffed and taken away. We have a new recruit in uniform now. His name is Abdul Rahman Abunasir. He is from Syria...think. He is eager to escort you to prison, and will see that you are comfortably settled in your new cell. But, before you submit to his handcuffs, I advise you to wear a headscarf to cover your hair and wear an ankle-length skirt.

Otherwise, he might be provoked and get mad at you…or something.

I am not a dumb person, young lady. There isn't anything I don't know. Sergeant Schultz at your service! Deaf to your screams, blind to your suffering, and mute on policy! I cannot stop those Muslims from raping you. It would be wrong to interfere with their religious duty! Have you no heart for them? Let them enrich your body with their sweat and seed! You'll grow to love the experience, I'm sure, and ask for more. Aren't they always saying that uncovered girls like you are "asking for it"? Of course, if you don't resist strongly enough, the court will say your rape was consensual and not rape at all. But if you scratch the fellow's face he might beat you unconscious, and disfigure you in the bargain. Just stop the screaming, please, and let me have my schnapps in peace!

https://edwardcline.blogspot.com/2016/02/sergeant-schultz-knows-everything.html

Friday, November 27, 2015

Chapter 8: Slandering the Prophet

Wiley E. Coyote as Mohammad chasing a Jew he found
hiding behind, first, a Gharkad tree, then behind a rock.
(*Hadith*, Sahih Muslim Book 041, Number 6985)

"The future must not belong to those who slander the prophet of Islam. But to be credible, those who condemn that slander must also condemn the hate we see in the images of Jesus Christ that are desecrated, or churches that are destroyed, or the Holocaust that is denied." President Barack Obama before the U.N. General Assembly, September 25, 2012.

It seems, to judge by his record before and after his U.N. address, in this instance that Obama delivered a verbose, sanctimonious dose of his golden-tongued *taqiyya* that mentioned desecrated images of Christ and Holocaust denial just so he couldn't be accused of bigotry or favoritism. However, he hasn't had much to say about the desecration and destruction of Christian and Jewish edifices and objects by ISIS, or by Islamic enthusiasts in Pakistan, Afghanistan, Malaysia, and in other culturally enriched Islamic pestholes.

On the other hand, it's fairly well known that Muslims can slander other creeds with legal and social impunity, and even publicly threaten death and dismemberment of anyone who slanders Mohammad and Islam or mentions them with a jaundiced eye.

But, how can you slander an icon, or a cartoon character, a fictional book, movie, or TV character, or a person who might not have even existed historically except in the minds of countless "believers" whose minds anyway are not too firmly anchored to reality? But perhaps it isn't the icon of Mohammad that should be slandered, mocked, and defamed, but those to whom the icon *is* a reality.

Those people actually exist. But you can't slander or libel someone whose existence a), has never been demonstrated except in the dubious assertive texts of an apocryphal "holy scripture" knocked together by two or three dozen "scholars" and tongue-in-cheek scribes over a thousand years; and b), whose physical appearance is unknown, nay, forbidden, under penalty of death. Mohammad left no dental records for forensics specialists to examine, no DNA samples to put through comparative analyses, no real surviving artifacts or memorabilia of things he might have owned or handled. Where's the spear, the turban, the sword? His sandals? There's the Kaaba in Mecca, but that's been rebuilt a dozen times. Western and even Persian artists over the centuries have produced an encyclopedia of depictions of Mohammad's physical appearance.

Is the Muslim belief in the holiness of Mohammad and the existence of Allah so tenuous, so shaky, so precarious that *any* slander or libel of them can precipitate a desperate, quivering, emotional outburst of anger? Are Muslims so addled that questions about Mohammad and Allah threaten the insular, super-sensitized mindset of the faithful? I have yet to encounter a Christian or a Jew who blew up at me for the suggestion that God and the Bible or the Torah might be ripping good fiction but otherwise are age-old figments of the imagination.

Of course, I could pose the same questions about the Christian and Judaic Jesus, but then Christians and Jews aren't threatening to kill me if I don't convert to their creeds. I could mock the idea of Moses parting the waters of the Red Sea and the antecedents of the Shroud of Turin, but I needn't fear for my life. Jews and Christians wouldn't be out to remove me from this mortal coil. They might not invite me to dinner, or they might curse my name in private, but that would be the extent of their persecution of me.

Alfred E. Neuman as Mohammad of Arabia

It's only adherents to the Islamic creed who behave like raving tyrants and homicidal maniacs every time someone gives Mohammad a raspberry shower or a scholarly vetting. And Islam cadged not only Jesus to add to its pantheon of "prophets," but other Biblical characters, as well. Finally, Allah was a moon god appropriated from a pagan creed. Given enough time and a little imagination, Mohammad and his successors might have chosen Steamboat Willie, otherwise known as Mickey Mouse, to be their all-merciful and all-powerful deity. However:

There is absolutely no question that Allah was worshipped by the pagan Arabs as one of many polytheistic gods. Allah was worshipped in the Kabah at Mecca before Muhammad was born. Muhammad merely proclaimed a god the Meccans were already familiar with. The pagan Arabs never accused Muhammad of preaching a different Allah than the one they already worshipped.

Many scholars say "Allah" is derived from a compound Arabic word, AL + ILAH = Allah. "Ilah" in Arabic is "God" and "Al" in Arabic is a definite article like our word "the". So from an English equivalent "Allah" comes from "The + God". Others, like Arthur Jeffery say, "The common theory is that it is formed from ilah, the common word for a god, and the article al-; thus al-ilah, the god," becomes Allah, "God." This theory, however, is untenable. In fact, the name is one of the words borrowed into the language in pre-Islamic times from Aramaic." (Islam: Muhammad and His Religion, Arthur Jeffery, 1958, p 85)

The article, "The pagan origin of the word "Allah," goes on to reveal:

It is not related that the Black Stone was connected with any special god. In the Ka'ba was the statue of the god Hubal who might be called the god of Mecca and of the Kaa'ba. Caetani gives great prominence to the connection between the Ka'ba and Hubal. Besides him, however, al-Lat, al-'Uzza, and al-Manat were worshipped and are mentioned in the Kur'an; Hubal is never mentioned there. What position Allah held beside these is not exactly known. The Islamic tradition has certainly elevated him at the expense of other deities. It may be considered certain that the Black Stone was not the only idol in or at the Ka'ba. The Makam Ibrahim was of course a sacred stone from very early times. Its name has not been handed down. Beside it several idols are mentioned, among them the 360 statues. (First Encyclopedia of Islam, E.J. Brill, 1987, Islam, p. 587-591)

"The verses of the Qur'an make it clear that the very name Allah existed in the Jahiliyya or pre-Islamic Arabia. Certain pagan tribes believed in a god whom they called 'Allah' and whom they believed to be the creator of heaven and earth and holder of the highest rank in the hierarchy of the gods. It is well known that the Quraish as well as other tribes believed in Allah, whom they designated as the 'Lord of the House' (i.e., of the Ka'ba)...It is therefore clear that the Qur'anic conception of Allah is not entirely new." (A Guide to the Contents of the Qur'an, Faruq Sherif, (Reading, 1995), pgs. 21-22., Muslim)

I could also slander Karl Marx and his "religion" of Communism, and Hitler and Nazism's central belief system. Well, okay, the Socialist and Communist might retort, Socialism and Communism have ruined every nation in which it's been tried, and resulted in the impoverishment, starvation, enslavement, and deaths of millions, but it can work if only we could produce the perfect Socialist or Communist man in the masses who could make it work. The Nazis had the same contention. And this explains why state control over education is so necessary to Socialists and Communists. Children and adolescents and grown adults must be mentally "conditioned" to labor with the most altruist spirit to sustain that ideal polity.

Mohammad in disguise as Georgetown University Professor of Islamic Studies, John Esposito

The "reality" of Mohammad and Allah seems to congeal into a pandemic gestalt whenever a Muslim prays. I mentioned this state of mind in a previous column.

Islam prohibits almost every pleasure. If a supernatural belief prevents a person from indulging in pleasures, then this belief also relieves this person of the guilt. And when the person is relieved of his guilt and shame because of this belief, his conviction that this belief is 'genuine' is consolidated. This re-enforces the validity of this belief in the person's mind on a constant basis. He feels 'pure', clean about himself as a result, while those who indulge in pleasure, appear 'filthy', dirty to him.

Compounding this phenomenon are the Islamic prayer gestures. While a Muslim is engaged in pretentious bodily movements and gestures of the Islamic prayer, his brain is subjected to a trance like state, which resonates with his desire to believe in a god, thereby again re-enforcing the notion that this belief is genuine, and is making him a better human being with each prayer.

A particular part of the human brain plays a critical role in this phenomenon. This part gives rise to a thirst for supernatural connection, which is quenched by Islam, and hence manipulates and motivates the person psychologically toward believing in Islam. This feel-good factor acts as the psychological impetus behind him being attached to Islam. He now clings on to Islam, because Islam makes him feel better about himself. Hence this person is motivated to keep practicing Islam, continue being delusional and keep following the imaginary Allah. Even kill in his name.

This is the secret behind the success of Islam.

And this is as close as any Muslim will ever come to Allah and his right-hand enforcer, Mohammad: by literally losing his "self" in a trance, by submitting to some kind of Islamic "rapture," by suspending his consciousness and his mind. It matters not if he erases himself privately or in a mass arse-liftings on Madison Avenue or Fleet Street or the Avenue des Champs-Élysées. When he's in this state, he's in that gestalt.

And this is as close as any Muslim will ever come to Allah and his right-hand enforcer, Mohammad: by literally losing his "self" in a trance, by submitting to some kind of Islamic "rapture," by suspending his consciousness and his mind. It matters not if he erases himself privately or in a mass arse-liftings on Madison Avenue or on Fleet Street or on the Avenue des Champs-Élysées. When he's in this state, he's in that gestalt.

What is a gestalt? *Merriam-Webster*'s definition of it is:

> **1.** Psychology : something that is made of many parts and yet is somehow more than or different from the combination of its parts; *broadly* : the general quality or character of something

> **2.** A structure, configuration, or pattern of physical, biological, or psychological phenomena so integrated as to constitute a functional unit with properties not derivable by summation of its parts

> *E Pluribus Ummah.* From the many, one.

You, Abdul, are nothing. We are all. So says the Islamic Ummah. We are the Borg.

How does a Muslim know Allah exists, that Islam is "true," and that Mohammad is the "Prophet"? Through his feelings. Sensory perception plays no role in this "knowledge."

How do you calmly discuss the delusions of Islam and Marxism with a Muslim and a Marxist without getting your head chopped off? How do you make any progress in persuading a Muslim and a Marxist that their ideologies are evil and even self-contradictory?
You don't. And you can't...a correspondent remarked after watching Stephen Coughlin's video version of *Catastrophic Failure: Blindfolding America in the Face of Jihad*:

The Marxists and Islamists are working in tandem to bring us down. Coughlin goes into detail on that issue, including how "political correctness" works to undermine the law of non-contradiction in those who fall prey to it. One section of his video briefing is titled "Interfaith Dialogue and the War on Reason". As the Marxists destroy the philosophical basis of the culture and the culture continues to disintegrate, the Muslims step in to offer an alternative to "truth" and "order", as the Nazis did in Weimar Republic Germany.

Au contraire, Mr. Obama. The future belongs to me and everyone else who values freedom of thought and of speech. If Muslims and Islam can't take criticism or mockery or slander, perhaps they should get out of the kitchen.

https://edwardcline.blogspot.com/2015/11/slandering-prophet.html

Saturday, November 14, 2015

Chapter 9: Raping the Swedish Corpse

"Merciful" Allah permits and encourages merciless rape *jihad*
...and this is the Swedes' reward, becoming prey to savages.

Gatestone ran a comprehensive report on the state of Sweden under the press of tens of thousands of immigrants, most of whom who have neither an affinity for Sweden nor a fondness for Swedes, except as prey for rape, robbery, and mayhem. The article, "Sweden descending into anarchy," of November 13th, by Ingrid Carlqvist, recounts the alarm Swedes are now feeling as the consequence of their government inviting countless barbarians into the country are becoming manifest. The reality of multiculturalism is hitting home, and hard.

But while reading Carlqvist's article, I couldn't help but remember that the Somali immigrant who raped a dying woman in a hotel garage, and then proceeded to rape her corpse, won't be deported after he has served his sentence. Once he's released, he is sure rape again, and commit other crimes. Why won't he be deported? Janna Brock wrote in 2013:

> It was early in the morning of 27 September. Police received an alarm that the two men were having intercourse with a woman who was completely unconscious on the floor of a parking garage under the Sheraton Hotel in Vasagatan in Stockholm.

When police arrived at the scene they found a 34 year old man from Somalia, who was in the midst of an anal intercourse with the woman. Police checked the woman's pulse and found that she was dead. The police caught the 34-year-old Somali Islamist in the act of brutally violating a corpse. What was he arrested for? It doesn't get more disgusting than this, but in Sweden one must not assume the man was guilty of murder.

The man was arrested by police and detained two days later by the Stockholm District Court, on suspicion of aggravated rape. The prosecutor had asked for him to be arrested for murder, but the district court found that the evidence for the suspicion was not strong enough.

Janna Brock, in a Freedom Outpost report, wrote:

The woman had minute traces of alcohol, cocaine, and prescription drugs in her body. But she was not dead at the time of the rape. The Somali Islamist claims the act was consensual. So the man in this consensual act continues to rape the woman after she is dead? This is depraved, but the Swedish judicial system is blind to the truth. They don't see this monster for what he is. Prosecutor Daniel Jonsson cited the death as an "abuse-related accident." Is this some kind of a sick joke?

The Swedish judicial system won't see him as a monster because to see him that way would be tantamount to politically incorrect *thoughtcrime*. When Prosecutor Jonsson was asked why he would not pursue the illegal immigrant's deportation after completing his prison sentence, he answered:

When Free Times asked if he, Jonsson, in light of the risk that the 34-year-old will commit more rapes in Sweden, still does not feel he has a responsibility to try and get the man deported, he answered no. "I do not understand why a Somali woman would be worth less than a Swedish woman in this context. He would be as likely to commit crimes there if he was deported.

In short, the life of a hypothetical Somali woman in a pesthole is more valuable to a Swedish prosecutor than the life of any Swedish woman, a fellow citizen. Or perhaps of equal value. The criminal might strike again in Somali. This cowardly prevarication, in practice, represents the nullification of *any* value, anywhere. We can't deport the savage because he might hurt someone else thousands of miles beyond Sweden's jurisdiction and realm of responsibility. But, we have an altruistic responsibility to protect everyone, everywhere, even if it is far from the aegis of civilized law.

What makes such a craven absurdity possible is – and I've discussed this point in past columns – Immanuel Kant's categorical imperative to "just do it," regardless of the cost to oneself or to anyone else. I've discussed this in both Parts of "The Mental States of the Political Elite," in "Pax Germania vs. Pax Islamia," and "The Know Nothings."

As Ingrid Carlqvist writes, the Swedes are just now realizing that their government has betrayed them, lied to them, and is unable or unwilling to protect them from the countless predators let into the country to avail themselves of the welfare state Swedes heretofore didn't think they would need to share with anyone else.

> Many Swedes see the mass immigration as a forced marriage: Sweden is forced to marry a man she did not choose, yet she is expected to love and honor him, even though he beats her and treats her badly. Her parents (the government) tell her to be warm and show solidarity with him.

In Sharia law, that's the Muslim male's primitive concept of marriage in practice. A wife is mere chattel to be used and beaten at will without consequence. Why should that concept not be extended to a whole population, to a whole country? The Muslim male expects unswerving devotion and service from his wife. Why should not that expectation be extended to all Swedes? Or to all Germans? Or to all Frenchmen. Or to all Americans?

Once upon a time, there was a safe welfare state called Sweden, where people rarely locked their doors. Now, this country is a night-watchman state -- each man is on his own. When the Minister of Justice, Morgan Johansson, encourages breaking the law, it means opening the gates to anarchy. Mr. and Mrs. Swede have every reason to be worried, with the influx of 190,000 unskilled and unemployed migrants expected this year -- equivalent to 2% of Sweden's current population....

And the Swedes are preparing: demand for firearms licenses is increasing; more and more Swedes are joining shooting clubs and starting vigilante groups. After a slight dip in 2014, the number of new gun permits has gone up significantly again this year. According to police statistics, there are 1,901,325 licensed guns, owned by 567,733 people, in Sweden. Add to this an unknown number of illegal weapons. To get a gun permit in Sweden, you need to be at least 18 years old; law-abiding; well-behaved, and have a hunting license or be a member of an approved shooting club. In 2014, 11,000 people got a hunting license: 10% more than the year before. One out of five was a woman.

But, in Sweden, as in Britain, there's a catch to arming oneself and defending oneself against predators. As a salesman for a Swedish security company relates about the skyrocketing demand for alarm systems:

"It is largely due to the turbulence we are seeing around the country at the moment." People have lost confidence in the State, he added. "The police will not come anymore. Truck drivers say that when they see a thief emptying the fuel tank of their trucks, they run out with a baseball bat. It is no use calling the police, but if you hit the thief, you can at least prevent him from stealing more diesel. Many homeowners say the same thing: they sleep with a baseball bat under the bed. *But this is risky: the police can then say you have been prepared to use force, and that might backfire on you." [Italics* mine.]

Being prepared to answer force with force can be punishable in a Swedish court? A Swede defending his home or his wife or family risks judicial penalties, but the initiator of force – the burglar, the thief, the rapist – incurs little or no penalty? But Sweden doesn't have a monopoly on stupidity. A British trucker was nearly jailed in Britain for carrying a "stun gun" in his cab to protect himself from marauding migrants in Calais.

A datable Muslim ?

But the Swedish news media and government will also punish those who speak out against the invasion of countless barbarians. Their policy is to cover up the dire seriousness of the crisis, so that their subjects can live in the same Fantasy Land. In Germany, if they can't cover up the resistance to Angela Merkel's policies, they shut it down with raids. As in Germany, the Swedish police are complicit in the cover-up of rapes, robberies, and terror Muslim gangs commit regularly.

Carlqvist goes on:

Even before the massive influx of migrants in the
fall of 2015, Swedes felt a need to protect
themselves -- and with good reason. Since the
Parliament decided in 1975 that Sweden should be
multicultural and not Swedish, crime has exploded.
Violent crime has increased by more than 300%,
and rapes have increased by an unbelievable
1,472%.

The politicians, however, ignore the people's fear
completely. It is never discussed. Instead, the
people who express concern about what kind of
country Sweden has become are accused of
xenophobia and racism. Most likely, that is the
reason more and more people are taking matters
into their own hands, and protecting themselves and
their families to the best of their ability.

But the highlight of Carlqvist's article was this revealing gem
uttered by Sweden's prime minister.

At a meeting with the Nordic Council in Reykjavik, Iceland, on
October 27, Sweden's Prime Minister, Stefan Löfven, was
questioned by his Nordic colleagues about the situation in
Sweden. Löfven had recently said that, "We should have the
option of relocating people applying for asylum in Sweden to
other EU-countries. Our ability, too, has a limit. We are facing a
paradigm shift." That comment led a representative of Finland's
Finns Party (*Sannfinländarna*) to wonder, with a hint of irony,
how mass immigration to Sweden, which for years Swedish
politicians have touted as being so profitable, has now suddenly
become a burden.

Still, in the face of his country's social collapse into anarchy
brought on by the immigrant invasion – and specifically by the
Muslim investiture of his country as an army of occupation – the
prime minister doubled down on his categorical imperative:

When Löfven was asked how he is dealing with the real concerns and demands of the citizenry, his answer was laconic: "Of course I understand there is concern," Löfven said. "It is not easy. But at the same time -- there are 60 million people on the run. This is also about them being our fellow men, and I hope that viewpoint will prevail."

Given the rising number of attacks on asylum centers by Swedish "vigilantes," that viewpoint looks like it's being shredded into confetti.

The daily tabloid *Expressen* asked Löfven about the attacks on asylum facilities. He replied, "Our communities should not be characterized by threats and violence, they should be warm and show solidarity."

Löfven and his ilk throughout Europe – and even in the U.S. – think that by showing "warmth and solidarity" with the parasites and predators, the latter will magically become hamsters and gerbils happily exercising in their spinning wheels.

I end this column here. The massive Jihadist/ISIS attack on Paris last night, November 13th, is monopolizing my energy and attention. President Barack Obama has made a statement of consolation that sounds more like a sympathetic, almost congratulatory message to ISIS, the Muslim Brotherhood, and other Islamic terror groups. He sounded almost regretful that the destruction in Paris wasn't wider and the casualties higher.

That's worth another column.

https://edwardcline.blogspot.com/2015/11/raping-swedish-corpse.html

Sunday, October 25, 2015

Chapter 10:   Pax Germania vs. Pax Islamia

ROBERT
HARRIS
Fatherland

Cover of the first UK edition, 1992, which
not so subtly pairs the Nazi and EU flags.

In the 1994 TV movie, *Fatherland*, Germany is depicted as
having won World War II, at least on the European continent,
which now has been consolidated into a single political entity,
Germania, or the Greater German Reich, stretching from the
Mediterranean to Finland (see a summary of the story here).

DVD Cover for the TV movie version
of Robert Harris's Fatherland

G3In April 1964, Germania is preparing to celebrate Hitler's
75th birthday. By 1964 standards, Berlin looks prosperous and
completely rebuilt after the failed Allied bombing. A former
German U-Boat commander, played by Rutger Hauer, now is a
top detective in the criminal division of an SS that resembles a
uniformed FBI. He investigates a murder which ultimately leads
to his discovery of a cover-up of the Nazi "final solution": that

all the Jews were exterminated, though the government maintains the fiction that they were all "resettled" in Russian territory conquered from the U.S.S.R.

At the same time, Hitler has persuaded President Joseph P. Kennedy to pay a "reconciliation" call in Germania and meet with him. The discovery of the "resettlement" fiction and of a series of murders of the Nazis responsible for the Holocaust would squelch any amicable relations between the U.S. and Germania. The still operative Gestapo goes to work to silence anyone who would be able to jeopardize that "peace process," beginning with the murders of all the Nazi higher-ups who took part in the Wannsee Conference. All these men had to die because they otherwise could have spilled the beans to the Americans about what really happened to the Jews – or at least blackmailed the Nazi government.

I have watched the TV movie and read Robert Harris's 1992 novel on which the TV movie is loosely based. They both err in several key ways in the "alternative history" genre, and the storylines of the novel and the movie also diverge at critical points. But two aspects of both the novel and the movie, however, I found incredible even as projected "alternative histories." They are, first, that the U.S.S.R. would have survived long enough to fight Hitler in a guerilla war in Eastern Russia clear up to 1964; in fact, it survived thanks to the aid FDR sent it, often at the expense of not equipping our own forces during WWII; and, second, that Joseph P. Kennedy would have been very rattled and outraged by the discovery that the Nazis had actually sent all the European Jews "up in smoke. Kennedy hated Jews almost as much as he hated the British.

After all, it was his belief that if the Nazis could not be appeased enough and if war broke out, the Jews were to be blamed, consequently scuttling plans to develop pacific relations and commercial ties with Nazi Germany. Kennedy also hated the British, but that's another story.

Those caveats were in the way of wading into the subject, not of *Pax Germania*, but of *Pax Islamia*.

Apparently Germany – and also Europe – is to be dominated and policed, not by clean-cut, close-shaven, neatly-outfitted by Hugo Boss, Führer-saluting Nazi brutes, but instead by not so clean, slovenly garbed, bearded, fist-shaking, Shahada-reciting Allah-worshipping brutes. Or by Muslims, whose immigrating cousins and nephews are already being called by native Germans and others "Nazis" because of their behavior and airs of superiority over native non-Muslims. The symbiosis between Nazi and Islamic ideologies has been well-documented, so this startling reversal of events should not come as a surprise to anyone.

Angela Merkel's plan to "unify" Europe vis-à-vis the resettling throughout Europe, by force or by extortion or by naked property expropriation, the uncounted hundreds of thousands of "refugees," "asylum-seekers," and other migrants from the Mideast, Africa, and other pestholes, bears strong similarities to Hitler's plans for Europe. Had Hitler won the war, or at least have emerged from it via a cease-fire or truce, he would have been able to follow his plan of *Lebensraum*, or to create (or seize) more "living space" for Germans.

Now, because of that symbiosis between Nazism and Islamism or Islamic supremacist doctrine, I don't think it's too ironic that Merkel wishes to turn the tables and be the enabler of the Muslim Brotherhood's general plan for conquering Europe (and the U.S.) by finding more "living space" for Muslims, and mandating it through the European Union.

It's not for nothing that Geert Wilders compared Hitler's *Mein Kampf* with the *Koran*.

The British Guardian, a left-leaning newspaper, carried in spite of itself a detailed, accurate description of how Merkel want to provide *Lebensraum* (in Arabic, مساحة eht ot (شة يـمـعـالMuslims, in Ian Traynor's October 23rd article, "Germany to push for compulsory EU quotas to tackle refugee crisis."

> Germany is to push for more ambitious and extensive common European Union policies on the refugee crisis, according to policymakers in Berlin, with compulsory and permanent quotas for sharing the distribution of probably hundreds of thousands of people who will arrive directly from the Middle East.

> Also on Berlin's agenda are new European powers replacing some national authority over border control, and the possible raising of a special EU-wide levy to fund the policies.

"Push" was the right verb to use. Chancellor Merkel, as head of Europe's largest and most prosperous nation, can be pushy. But, if Germany is willing to make itself miserable by welcoming hundreds of thousands of welfare-seekers, the misery must be spread around. It's only fair that others suffer, as well.

Angela Merkel appears determined to prevail, as she grapples with a crisis that will likely define her political legacy. The German chancellor is said to be angry with the governments of eastern and central Europe which are strongly opposed to being forced to take in refugees. She is said to resent that these EU member states are pleading for "solidarity" against the threats posed by EU government leaders agreed last month to share responsibility for 160,000 asylum seekers already in the EU, redistributing them from Greece and Italy over two years.

But the decision had to be pushed to a majority vote, overruling the dissenters, mainly in eastern Europe, and with the Hungarian prime minister, Viktor Orban, accusing Merkel of "moral imperialism." It is highly unusual in the EU for sensitive issues with such deep national political impact to be settled by majority voting. But Berlin appears prepared to do this if no consensus can be reached.

The dissenters had to be overruled, especially those who don't wish to see their countries despoiled by hordes of barbarians prone to riot, rape and robbery. Imperialism? Eastern Europeans have already had a taste of German and Soviet imperialism, so they can't be blamed for not wanting another round of it.

The opponents of quotas insist last month's decision was a one-off. But according to policymakers in Berlin, Merkel now wants to go further, shifting the emphasis of burden-sharing from redistribution of refugees inside the EU to those collecting en masse in other countries, notably Turkey, where more than 2 million Syrians are being hosted.

Under one proposal being circulated in Berlin, the EU would strike pacts with third countries, such as Turkey, agreeing to take large but unspecified numbers of refugees from them directly into Europe. In return, the third country would need to agree on a ceiling or a cap for the numbers it can send to Europe and commit to keeping all other migrants and refugees, and accommodate them humanely. This effectively means Europe would be financing large refugee camps in those third countries, which will also be obliged to take back any refugees who are not granted asylum in Europe.

Turkey? The same Turkey run by Recep Tayyip Erdoğan, an Islamic supremacist who dreams of a new Ottoman Empire, who proclaimed that "Mosques are our barracks, minarets our bayonets, domes our helmets, the believers our soldiers"? Yes, *that* authoritarian tyrant. Birds of a feather, indeed.

> Merkel returned from talks on the issue with the Turkish leadership on Sunday seemingly convinced that Ankara was the key to her winning some relief on the toxic immigration issue. She is being criticized for ignoring human rights problems in her dealings with Turkey's authoritarian leader, President Recep Tayyip Erdoğan. But according to people familiar with her thinking, she has concluded that, in terms of Turkey, the main third country source of migrants heading for Europe, interests trump values.

Principles? Values? They can be dispensed with. Turkey has always wanted to become part of the European Union and what better way to join it than striking a deal with the Crazy Kraut Kaffir? Shades of the Molotov–Ribbentrop "non-aggression pact" of 1939! An inconvenient historical fact that Merkel doubtless doesn't choose to remember.

Fatherland's 1964 Europe, as imagined by Robert Harris. Or, *Mutterland*'s 2016 Europe, the Greater German Reich, as imagined by Weiblicher Führer Angela Merkel.

The plans being developed in Berlin and Brussels also include moves to "Europeanize" control of the EU's external borders. This would entail national governments surrendering some of their powers on those frontiers and granting at least some authority over refugee admissions, detentions and deportation to EU bodies such as Frontex, the fledgling borders agency.

Some senior diplomats and officials in Brussels say this is an intrusion into national sovereignty which will be difficult for some governments to accept. Policymakers in Berlin are aware of the sensitivities, but appear of a mind to proceed by stealth in small steps.

There is always lots of play in a noose before it's tightened around one's neck. The trick is to tighten it slowly, so as not to alarm the victim and cause him to gag beforehand. And the noose's knot *must* be a silken, Europeanized knot, the kind with which the British used to hang their aristocrats. Delusions among European leaders are the panacea of the day. Merkel can't really mean it! Oh, but she does.

Forced to bow to the sharing of 160,000 refugees last month, several EU leaders took the view that this was a limited and temporary move that would not be repeated. But for Berlin, it is but a beginning in the formulation of pan-European asylum and immigration policies.

On Wednesday Juncker called a Brussels summit for Sunday for some EU and Balkan leaders to tackle the crisis in Croatia, Slovenia, and Austria since Hungary closed its borders to those arriving in the EU from Turkey and Greece via the Balkans.

The German push for taking people directly from places such as Turkey has the merit of cutting out of many of the smuggling rackets prospering from the mass movements and reducing the numbers of those risking the hazardous journeys from the Middle East to the borders of Europe. But it is far from clear that the plan to persuade third-country governments to agree to enforce a ceiling on the numbers allowed to go to the EU can work.

And, here comes the tax to pay for the noose and the executioner.

Europe, courtesy of Mother Merkel

According to the thinking in Berlin, if the new package of policies must involve a European solution rather than a mish-mash of national strategies, it will also have to be financed at the European level, possibly through a special levy, since the billions involved would blow a gaping hole in the existing EU budget and national governments would balk at footing the bills.

Daniel Greenfield, in Sultan Knish, writes that Germany and other members of the EU want to retain their welfare states and eat the Muslims, too. In his brutally frank assessment of the future of Europe, "The Death of Europe" of October 23rd, he remarks:

European leaders talk about two things these days; preserving European values by taking in Muslim migrants and integrating Muslim migrants into Europe by getting them to adopt European values.

It does not occur to them that their plan to save European values depends on killing European values.

That's because Islamic values are diametrically opposite of European ones. Even the bad European ones, such as the Uncle Otto pays-for-everything welfare state including everyone's retirement plans, which include those of Muslims who never paid anything into the system and never intended to.

Europe invested in the values of its welfare state. The Muslim world invested in large families. Europe expects the Muslim world to bail out its shrinking birth rate by working and paying into the system so that its aging population can retire. The Muslim migrants however expect Europe to subsidize their large families with its welfare state while they deal some drugs and chop off some heads on the side....

The European values that require Europe to commit suicide are about ideology, not language, culture or nationhood. But the incoming migrants don't share that ideology. They have their own Islamic values.

Why should 23-year-old Mohammed work for four decades so that Hans or Fritz across the way can retire at 61 and lie on a beach in Mallorca? The idea that Mohammed would ever want to do such a thing out of love for Europe was a silly fantasy that European governments fed their worried citizens.

And now those same citizens are witnessing the fantasy colliding with reality. Greenfield's essay on why Europe has doomed itself ought to win some kind of journalistic award. But it won't. Greenfield concludes:

Islamic values are not compatible with European values. Not only free speech and religious freedom, but even the European welfare state is un-Islamic. Muslims have a high birth rate because their approach to the future is fundamentally different from the European one....

Europe is drinking rat poison to cure a cold. Instead of changing its values, it's trying to maintain them by killing itself. The Mohammed retirement plan won't save European Socialism.

It will bury it.

And Europe, as well. All that will be left will be ashes, ruins, and corpses underfoot of millions of Muslims looking for a new place to "migrate."

The United States.

https://edwardcline.blogspot.com/2015/10/pax-germania-vs-pax-islamia.html

Friday, September 11, 2015

Chapter 11: "There Was a Crooked House...."

A government arts grant applicant

There was a crooked man, and he walked a crooked mile,
He found a crooked sixpence against a crooked stile;
He bought a crooked cat which caught a crooked mouse,
And they all lived together in a little crooked house.
–Mother Goose

Our Cultural Establishment is all about crooked little men, getting and spending bags full of crooked sixpence, and own crooked cats which keep chasing crooked mice, in the National Endowment for the Arts, and in the National Endowment for the Humanities. These two organizations are populated with crooked little men and cash-flush caitiffs and assorted other denizens of the ongoing cultural scam with their crooked little smiles and crooked sixpence.

Have you ever wondered where all the trashy literature and modern anti-art comes from? Or, rather, have you ever scratched your head in wonder about who paid to have it produced? In large part, we, the taxpayers pay for it, through Federal, State, and local taxes. These unreadable, boring, super-naturalistic or unclassifiable novels, those "controversial" or shock-jock or feminist shock-crotch plays, the sculpture that looks like debris from the collapse of the World Trade Center on 9/11, the crucifixes in jars of urine, the welded-together auto parts, the cheapjack, hand-held camera movies one can find by the wheelbarrow-load on Netflix, each crediting half a dozen or more oddly-named production companies – these are also the products of private grant money.

Private sector grants are made annually in the billions of dollars. So, we can't blame the Federal, state, or local governments for everything that's rotten. The boards and selection committees of dozens of "charitable" foundations, big and small, are also responsible for littering the cultural landscape with consumable, throw-away rubbish.

This private grant business – or, I should say this private grant racket, as it's as much a racket as are all of the government's – together with the Federal government encourages, promotes, and enables mediocrity and the otherwise unsalable in the culture. The irrational, the sub-average, the hackneyed, and the prosaic passed off as "novel" or "radical" are the touchstones of virtue worthy of a lifetime sinecure, a prestigious teaching job, and lots of money. It is the practice of elevating the undistinguished distinguished only by their banality.

Government grants today are the whores' whelps of the Depression era Works Progress Administration (WPA) and the Federal Writers' Project (FWP). Their official progeny are the National Endowment for the Arts (NEA) and the National Endowment for the Humanities (NEH).

In sum, private and government grants have also turned fringe writers and artists into the foremost. Receiving a grant, fellowship, residency, or all-expenses-paid "quiet time" vacation at some artists' or writers' colony or community is one's official induction into the cultural establishment. For example, see this Wikipedia entry on one of the more famous "retreats," Yaddo:

Yaddo is an artists' community located on a 400-acre (1.6 km²) estate in Saratoga Springs, New York. Its mission is "to nurture the creative process by providing an opportunity for artists to work without interruption in a supportive environment."[1] On March 11, 2013 it was designated a National Historic Landmark.

It offers residencies to artists working in choreography, film, literature, musical composition, painting, performance art, photography, printmaking, sculpture, and video. Collectively, artists who have worked at Yaddo have won 66 Pulitzer Prizes, 27 MacArthur Fellowships, 61 National Book Awards, 24 National Book Critics Circle Awards, 108 Rome Prizes, 49 Whiting Writers' Awards, a Nobel Prize (Saul Bellow, who won the Pulitzer Prize in Fiction and Nobel Prize in Literature in 1976), and countless other honors.

There are even sites that promote the writing grant applications as a profession. Remember those matchbook correspondence school ads that asked if you wanted to become a painter or a medical billing expert or a dog handler, and "here's how"? These are the online equivalents of how to get started in writing government and private grant applications for yourself, for your community or business, or for others.

I began taking notes for this column to discuss PEN, and out of curiosity I went onto the PEN America Center site to see what writers – known to me and unknown – were members of this organization. There seemed to be hundreds of members – perhaps, I imagined, over a thousand. I tried counting them, but it would've taken me two mind-numbing hours to complete just one column of names and as a result would have grown cross-eyed. And there were *two* columns. I got through about 1/20th of just one column before calling it quits.

Then a PEN staffer answered my query about the number of living, dues-paying PEN members: "Roughly 4,200."

Red highlighted names are links to a writer's own blog site or to some program he is connected to or affiliated with. This double-columned list, which seems to go on for several scroll-downs, is just chock full of names of famous writers you have never heard of:

Such as: Paul LaFarge, Britt Leach, Linda Leavall, Russell Banks (Banks is better known), Joyce Carole Oates (also better known), Millicent Dillon, and Judy Blume. Ever hear of Belinda McKeon, Marie Mutsuki Mocket, Selene Castrovilla, Taiye Selasi, Norman Sprinrad, Samrat Upadhyay, Luis Alterto Urrea, Metta Sáma, or Sergio Troncoso? No? Don't you read? They're literary immortals.

Many of these writers are recipients of MacArthur and Guggenheim Foundation grants and "fellowships." The MacArthur Foundation is singular in its awards to some of the most ditzy "artists" and writers. The mission statement of the MacArthur Foundation goes:

Now led by President Julia Stasch, MacArthur is one of the nation's largest independent foundations with assets of approximately $6.3 billion and annual giving of approximately $220 million.

The Foundation supports creative people and effective institutions committed to building a more just, verdant, and peaceful world. In addition to selecting the MacArthur Fellows, the Foundation works to defend human rights, advance global conservation and security, make cities better places, and understand how technology is affecting children and society.

The Guggenheim Foundation's purpose is similar in ends and means:

United States Senator Simon Guggenheim and his wife established the John Simon Guggenheim Memorial Foundation in 1925 as a memorial to a son who died April 26, 1922. The Foundation offers Fellowships to further the development of scholars and artists by assisting them to engage in research in any field of knowledge and creation in any of the arts, under the freest possible conditions and irrespective of race, color, or creed. The Foundation receives between 3,500 and 4,000 applications each year. Although no one who applies is guaranteed success in the competition, there is no prescreening: all applications are reviewed. Approximately 200 Fellowships are awarded each year.

About those Guggenheim Fellowships, here is a clue:

Often characterized as "midcareer" awards, Guggenheim Fellowships are intended for men and women who have already demonstrated exceptional capacity for productive scholarship or exceptional creative ability in the arts.

Fellowships are awarded through two annual competitions: one open to citizens and permanent residents of the United States and Canada, and the other open to citizens and permanent residents of Latin America and the Caribbean. Candidates must apply to the Guggenheim Foundation in order to be considered in either of these competitions.

Not a money-maker, but a money-getter

I've seen some of the "productive scholarship" the Guggenheim subsidizes. It's on a par with "The History and Social Status of Maori Tattooing Arts," while much of the "exceptional creative ability" sustained by the Foundation is along the lines of the notorious ribbon fence in California. See also the works of Robert Mapplethorpe, Andres Serrano, and Richard Serra.

Many, many MacArthur, Guggenheim and other foundation "fellows" are "double dippers," that is, they are recipients of both government and private grants. To wit:

Anthony Cerulli's next project, *Sanskrit Medical Classics in Crisis: Language Politics and the Reinvention of a Medical Tradition in India*, which he will pursue as a Guggenheim Fellow, explores the impact of European colonial medicine on the transmission of knowledge in one of India's classical medical traditions, Ayurveda....

Cerulli has been the recipient of fellowships from the American Council of Learned Societies, European Institutes for Advanced Study, Fulbright Foundation, and National Endowment for the Humanities. He has held appointments as Directeur d'études invité at the École des hautes études en sciences sociales in Paris, Chercheur invité at the Institut d'études avancées in Paris, and twice as scholar-in-residence at the Rochester Zen Center in western New York. Since 2008, he has taught at Hobart and William Smith Colleges, where he is Associate Professor of Religious Studies and Asian Studies. Since 2009, he has been the Managing Editor of the journal *India Review*.

PEN (comprising of PEN International and PEN World) opposes censorship and champions the freedom of speech of many foreign writers jailed or persecuted by their governments. Its mission statement reads:

International PEN, the worldwide association of writers, was founded in 1921 to promote friendship and intellectual cooperation among writers everywhere; to emphasize the role of literature in the development of mutual understanding and world culture; to fight for freedom of expression; and to act as a powerful voice on behalf of writers harassed, imprisoned, and sometimes killed for their views.

PEN is strictly non-political, a non-governmental organization in formal consultative relations with UNESCO and Special Consultative Status with the Economic and Social Council of the United Nations.

PEN is composed of Centers, each of which represents its membership and not its country, and membership of its Centers is open to all qualified writers, journalists, translators, historians, and others actively engaged in any branch of literature, regardless of nationality, race, colour or religion. Every member is required to sign the PEN Charter and by so doing to observe its conditions.

PEN is supported by a Mulligan stew of major corporations and government agencies, including the NEA and the Open Society Institute (the latter is a George Soros creation to help bring about Obama's "transformed America"). But PEN can't be "strictly non-political" if is associated with the United Nations, with the Open Society Institute, with the Ford Foundation, and with other left-wing "charitable" entities.

PEN's overall opposition to censorship and restrictions on freedom of speech may be commendable, but it is a policy which operates in a moral and intellectual vacuum. There are some thirty PEN affiliates in various countries. It views freedom of speech as an intrinsic value that ought to thrive in any political context, and as a "right" that should be respected irrespective of the character of a country's political system. It is a "floating abstraction." Without property rights, there can be no freedom of speech. If a government owns or controls all venues of expression, then demanding that it guarantee its citizens freedom of speech is whistling into the wind.

On a personal note, I would not be invited to join PEN, nor would I be able to receive any kind of grant, government or private, even if I applied for one, because my fiction has no "edge." It's not "mainstream." It performs no discernible or definable "social good." It wasn't written as a "community service." It would probably be deemed "violent," "homophobic," "sexist," and perhaps even "old-fashioned," "creativity famished," and even "Islamophobic."

No, this is not a "sour grapes" column. I haven't written it because I've been overlooked or ignored by today's cultural establishment and wish to send a zinger to PEN or any other leftward cultural organization. My name and book titles are not household words in the homes of establishment critics. I'd be unwelcome in any secular synod of contemporary writers and artists.

Frankly, I'm grateful that I've been ignored or rendered invisible in today's culture. I'd rather be known for the company I keep, and that's all my fans and loyal readers, and friends.

https://edwardcline.blogspot.com/2015/09/there-was-crooked-house.html

Tuesday, April 7, 2015

Chapter 12: Political Cinema

Returning after another hiatus, during which I finished the ninth Cyrus Skeen detective novel (*The Circles of Odin*), I decided not to try and recap all the bad news about Islam, Obama, Europe, and the decrepit state of the economy and, of the government that came our way over the last two months, but instead to pen a spate of TV/movie reviews. These, too, however, are mostly bad news.

Keeper of the Flame

The only semi-bright spot in the reviews is one about *Keeper of the Flame*, a film I had for years wanted to see. I was intrigued by the title. I finally made the time to watch it on Amazon Instant Video. The Amazon Books entry on the novel by I.A.R. Wylie on which the film was based, features a book cover and a still from the movie, with stars Katherine Hepburn and Spencer Tracy. But because that listing does not allow one to "open the book to look inside," I had no idea at the time if the cover hid the original novel, or if the book was a novelization of the film.

An Internet search for Wylie and the book turned up this explanation by an anonymous enthusiast on the Neglected Books site. It answered my question:

> This Popular Library edition of I. A. R. Wylie's 1942 novel, Keeper of the Flame, dates from the early 1960s. There are some remarkable titles to be found among the best-sellers, bodice-rippers, and dreck that Popular Library released in the late 1950s and early 1960s. I wrote about a few of them about a year ago in the post, Digging into the Popular Library at the Montana Valley Book Store."

> This is a particularly odd example. MGM purchased the film rights to Keeper of the Flame when the book was still unpublished. It was then published by Random House before the film was released, but subsequent runs featured a dust jacket with a still shot from the movie.

> Aside from the unusual story, Keeper of the Flame– both the novel and the film–are far more interesting seen in the context of their external connections and references. One watches the film looking for hints of the budding attraction between Hepburn and Tracy. One reads the novel in light of the figures such as Charles Lindburgh {*sic*} and Father Coughlin who inspired popular movements in America in the 1930s and 1940s–movements we now see as having a darker side.

> Having written recently about Wylie's memoir, My Life with George, I was impressed by two aspects of the book. First, it's hard not to think that Wylie wrote it for the screen: there are at least a dozen scenes that play out exactly as filmed, and the whole sequence of the narrative matches that of the film so tightly it could have been a novelization

after the fact. Second, despite the many superficial and clichéd characterizations, it's obvious that Wylie was a very world-smart woman: if she played down her intelligence, it was because she'd had, by the 1940s, also thirty years' experience of making a living with her writing.

To judge by Amazon's book information, Grosset and Dunlap, not Random House, published Wylie's book in 1942 before the film was released.

The article has a link to a review of one of Wylie's other books (also by anonymous), *My Life with George*.

And what is *Keeper of the Flame* (the film) about?

Spencer Tracy plays Steven 'Stevie' O'Malley, a war correspondent who returns to the States to seek out the widow of Robert Forrest (a character who never appears in the film), an apparently charismatic war hero (WWI) who had risen as a powerful political force. Katherine Hepburn plays Christine Forrest, Forrest's widow. O'Malley, who admires Forrest and what he ostensively stood for, wants to write a "true" biography of Robert Forrest, and requests the help of his widow. Inexplicably, she is reluctant to help O'Malley perpetuate the memory of her late husband.

Forrest was killed in an accident when his car drove off a collapsed bridge during a thunder storm. O'Malley begins to suspect that Forrest's death was indeed caused by the collapsed bridge – and that no one tried to warn him about the bridge. I won't say much more about the plot. This is a well-made film, directed by George Cukor, boasting a top cast, and even if it was wartime propaganda (released by MGM in March 1943), it is well worth watching. It's rentable on Amazon Instant Videos. There are parallels in the overall theme that mesh with today's fascination with Barack Obama and how he has remained untouchable by the news media and the Left. Obama succeeded where Forrest did not.

However, the most important aspect of *Keeper of the Flame* was then and still is its political message: Some heroes become fascists. They advocate "Americanisms" which aren't really "Americanisms" but instead are crypto-values disguising the tenets of fascism, which are anti-democratic, anti-religion, anti-liberty, and even racist. Although many of the pro-democracy and pro-liberty sentiments expressed in the film are banal and clichéd, and on close examination, specious, I found it curious that Communism didn't come in for the same criticism. It seemed that no one in Hollywood realized that one can be enslaved or murdered by a hammer and sickle as effectively and permanently as by a swastika.

That was because Soviet Russia was an alleged ally, and orders came down from the Roosevelt administration that Hollywood was to refrain from any criticism of and "Uncle" Josef Stalin, even though it was known that the Soviet Union was as much a totalitarian hellhole as was Nazi Germany. Hollywood obeyed. It was okay to excoriate Hitler and Nazism (and even American heroes; many reader comments on the IMDB site voiced the suspicion that *Keeper of the Flame* was a *roman à clef* about Charles Lindberg, who was pro-Nazi), but not Stalin and his dictatorship.

For a compelling and an encyclopedic-documented exposé of the political atmosphere during WWII as relates to Hollywood and its self-censorship concerning the Soviet Union, see Diana West's *American Betrayal: The Secret Assault on Our Nation's Character*, which discusses, among other things (especially Soviet spies, American and Soviet), how FDR was basically Stalin's policy poodle when it came to fighting the war and painting an uncritical, benevolent face of Stalin and Communism (for American "morale" reasons). See also her column about Senator Joseph McCarthy, and M. Stanton Evans's Breitbart article on how anyone questioning the copasetic relationship between FDR and Stalin was and still is mercilessly slandered, libeled, and misrepresented.

Mad Men

On someone's recommendation, I began watching *Mad Men* on Netflix when it debuted in that venue years ago. Season Seven, the very last season, has already debuted this month. But as time went by – and I watched the series only because of the ballyhoo surrounding it, so I figured it was a culturally significant series to watch – my yawns grew longer and louder. I always found the character of Don Draper, the chief "mad man," played by John Hamm (whom I guess would be regarded as a "hunk" to most women) not so much a mysterious character, as an ambiguous, amorphous, and extraordinarily shallow one. He was so dull and pedestrian that even, from the standpoint of disinterested prurience, his many graphically-portrayed episodes of promiscuity and philandering were yawners. His character was so bland that when he was angry and threw things around, one couldn't get excited.

Hamm's Don Draper invites one to redefine "average." His life and even his name were frauds, he was not particularly brilliant in devising advertising campaigns, his manner and motives were inscrutable, and he was so unexceptional a character that he never even left a bad taste in my mouth. He left no taste at all. One couldn't hate him. How can one hate a nonentity?

I stuck with the series, expecting the character to grow, but he remained stunted in a milieu of glamorous pragmatism. None of the other recurring characters in the series (and there are about three dozen) elicited the least sympathy or empathy in me. I think I watched the series from a sense of nostalgia for the

1960's, when the government and the Left had not yet clamped down on smoking, drinking, "truth in advertising," and unapologetically looking at women as sex objects – among other things the government now regulates or has something to say about. I also worked in New York City in the time in which the series is set, and for not a few advertising agencies, and recognized the landmarks and clothing and the hectic nature of the business.

Mad Men is naturalism taken to its basic, unembellished level. Purportedly, this was how life was back in the 1960s on Madison Avenue. And…? If this was a "slice of life," who would want it?

House of Cards

President Barack Obama and former president Bill Clinton have weighed in on the credibility of the Kevin Spacey *House of Cards*. Their statements about the American TV political series dramatizing the climb to power and the presidency by an amoral creature through murder, stealth, sacrificing others, and verisimilitude are not surprising, because both Obama and Clinton achieved power by the same means. Well, perhaps not by murder, but by employing a fleet of buses under which to throw their many victims, including the American people.

About half a century ago, President John F. Kennedy, not a man I admire by any means, confessed he liked Ian Fleming's James Bond novels, popular adventure literature that dramatized good vs. evil. Well into the 21st century a sitting president and a former president have expressed admiration for evil and its triumph. To date, that is the thematic essence of *House of Cards*.

Britain's Daily Mail on April 3rd reported on the twelve-second "selfie" (and that's all one could call it):

> President Barack Obama took a break from being the real president on April Fools' Day to impersonate a fictional one, House of Cards' conniving Frank Underwood. 'Hello everybody. This is not Frank Underwood,' the president said after turning his head Underwood, who is played by Oscar-winning actor Kevin Spacey and frequently speaks Shakespearean-style monologues to the audience. 'This is Barack Obama. Happy April Fools' Day. Frank learned it from me,' he said.

> He has previously admitted to watching the Netflix show, though he says that life in Washington is not as dramatic as portrayed by Kevin Spacey and others. 'I wish things were that ruthlessly efficient,' he said in 2013. The short clip in front of a portrait of Abraham Lincoln begins with a statement of the time and date, a commonly used scene entry device in House of Cards.

> Meanwhile, Bill Clinton confessed to Charlie Rose to being a House of Cards "binger," watching continuous episodes of it for days. The New York Daily News reported in August 2013:

> The former President told "Cards" star Kevin Spacey, "I love that show. It's so good," the actor revealed in a Charlie Rose interview that aired on Bloomberg this week.

> "We watched it over three days it was so good," he told Spacey about not having the forbearance to spread out his viewing.

I've reviewed the Spacey House of Cards on Rule of Reason here, here, here, and here.

I concluded *House of Cards*: A Post-Mortem in February 2014 with:

Ayn Rand, the novelist/philosopher, could solve such as paradox as the self-denigrating nature of "House of Cards" and note that:

"To the extent to which a man is rational, life is the premise directing his actions. To the extent to which he is irrational, the premise directing his actions is death."*

The whole of Frank Underwood's character is devoted to the irrational, and the irrationality he practices necessitates inflicting pain to acquire political power. He doesn't actually want to live; but neither does he want anyone else to survive his death-wish, either.

That is *nihilism.*

While the finale of Season 3 of *House of Cards* ended with an anti-climax – Claire, Underwood's wife, played by Robin Wright, has announced that she's leaving him just when he needs her to secure election, thus guaranteeing losing the election – Kevin Spacey has claimed that the series will run for twelve seasons.

The actor, who plays vice president-elect Frank Underwood going into the show's second series, once joked that the Netflix original production could go on for a mega 37 series – but has since had a bit of a change of heart. Quizzed on how long he thinks the show could go on for, he told Digital Spy: '12 years, 12 seasons.'

That's as bad and discouraging as predicting twelve more years of Barack Obama.

The Virtue of Selfishness, by Ayn Rand. 1964. New York: Signet. P. 25.

https://edwardcline.blogspot.com/2015/04/political-cinema.html

Tuesday, May 6, 2014

Chapter 13: Sharia for Dummies

No, that's not the actual title. *Sharia-ism is Here: The Battle to Control Women and Everyone Else* might have been called that but doubtless Joy Brighton, the author, would have encountered brand or trademark infringement problems with the publisher of the popular and successful *For Dummies* series, John Wiley & Sons. I also suspect that Wiley & Sons would have been horrified by the idea of publishing such an "Islamophobic" book anyway. It has published *Islam for Dummies* and *The Koran for Dummies*, both of which, to judge by their Amazon descriptions, are treacly, inoffensive, sanitized guides to a highly "misunderstood" and "misperceived" religion-cum-ideology.

Brighton's opus is a generously illustrated and annotated book intended as a "show n' tell book for national security, civil right and women's right activists and lobbyists in America." It is meant to be read by, and serve as, a handy reference guide for anyone who is aware of the peril posed by Islam as it is practiced around the world, in the West, and especially in the U.S., but who really hasn't digested the scale of the threat or any of its details. And it isn't just about Islam's crusade to control women. It truly is about Islam's designs on everyone.

Before citing the book's plenitude of virtues, however, there is one issue I must raise. Page 131, for example, under the heading, "Conversion to Islam or Sharia-ism in America? How do we help youth understand the difference?" highlights the conversion percentages of Americans to Islam. At the bottom of the page is an "Insight Box," which reads:

How many of these American Converts have been converted to Islam the religion? How many are knowingly or unknowingly slowly being converted to Sharia-ism, the political movement of Radical Islam? How do we help young potential converts understand the difference and draw the line between Islam and Sharia-ism?

One point of disagreement between *Sharia-ism is Here: The Battle to Control Women* and me is that I *do not* draw a line between Islam and what Brighton calls "Sharia-ism." Brighton writes in her Introduction:

You are holding in your hands a chronicle of the surprising inroads that Shariah, the guiding principles of Radical Islam, has made in America during the critical years of 2008-2013.

Radical Islam, also known as Political or Sharia Islam, has expanded onto every continent, and with it Sharia-ism, the political movement of Radical Islam, whose goal of totalitarian control of every nation and people is incompatible with Western values of individual liberties and inalienable rights. Sharia-ism is about politics, not religion.

Sharia-ism is about total control, not simply destruction or terrorism. (p. 6)

Both of Brighton's terms, *Sharia-ism* and *Radical Islam*, violate Ockham's Razor of economy of concepts by arbitrarily divorcing Islam and Sharia. The dichotomy is fallacious and inadvertently grants Islam an unsought-after epistemological and ideological victory. Brighton is not the only authority to commit this error. Seen as a virulent ideology, Islam and Sharia are one and the same. They are inherently complementary and co-dependent. I do not think Islam, "moderate" or otherwise, is a benign belief system, because it is fundamentally political, nihilist, and totalitarian in means and ends. Sharia is Islam, and Islam is nothing without Sharia. Without the primitive, anti-conceptual, rote-learned code of Sharia, Islam is little better, and perhaps even worse, than your random whacky California cult, or Scientology, Wiccanism, or Pyramid-Worship.

Further, were it not an ideology, why have its proponents, spokesmen, and activists focused so much on its political status? Catholics, Protestants, Jews and members of other creeds are not waging campaigns to force government, businesses, and other social organizations to accommodate their beliefs and practices. The promulgators of Islam, however, such as CAIR and the various Muslim organizations in this country, seek accommodations to Islam in virtually every sphere of American life, from demanding foot baths in various venues (schools, office buildings, airports), removing "offensive" crucifixes and other non-Islamic religious icons from classrooms, insisting on *halal* restaurant menus, to praying *en masse* on public streets, to inveigling their way into government jobs and appointments.

By way of contrast, I am not aware of a movement in the Catholic Church to compel, by statute, non-Catholics to genuflect when passing a Catholic church on the street, or else pay a fine.

And, perhaps more importantly in the context of politicizing Islam, Catholicism, Protestantism, Judaism, and other faiths do not campaign to silence critics and criticism of those faiths. Islam, however, yearns to suppress all criticism of its practices and tenets. As Brighton herself points out in her book, the term "Islamophobia" was coined by the Muslim Brotherhood to stigmatize any and all criticism of Islam, the term implying racial, ethnic, or religious bigotry.

Finally, even were one to portray Islam as a mere patriarchic theocracy, one is still talking politics, for a theocracy implies the governing moral structure of a country. Ergo, it is a political system, and specifically a totalitarian one, because it prescribes the course of one's life from head to foot, from sunrise to sunset, in thought, in action, and in one's social associations.

I make no allowances for Islam, or cut it any slack by calling it a "private" belief system as I might the Catholic or Jewish. *Privacy* is not Islam's leitmotif; on the contrary, it is unabashedly and necessarily *public*. Conformance to its bizarre catalogue of dictats is audited. Straying from the ritualistic and behavioral drill can result in death (e.g., honor killings, and for apostasy). To refer to "radical Islam" is to commit a redundancy. Islam is "radical" in the sense that must obviate all other alternatives and choices, else it is nothing. Force or the threat of force is Sharia's telling hand. Islam is Sharia, and *vice versa*.

"Passive," non-violent Muslims face a decision: a continuation of their submission to Islam, or total repudiation, as Ayaan Hirsi Ali decided on. There is no dignified or respectable "middle ground"; one cannot be half-free and free at the same time. That is a delusion. See some of my columns on Islam and its inherently totalitarian and irrational nature here, here, here, and here.

Those objections having been made, *Sharia-ism is Here* draws on a galaxy of authorities on Islam such as Nonie Darwish, Steve Emerson, Robert Spencer, Ayaan Hirsi Ali, Wafa Sultan, Walid Phares, Diana West, and Melanie Phillips, to name but a few whose names appear in the Acknowledgements and throughout the text.

There are fifteen chapters in the book, under such titles as "What is Sharia-ism and Shariah Islamic Law?"; "Sharia-ism: Concepts and Vocabulary"; two chapters, titled "Two-Armed Leadership of Sharia-ism," one dealing with Shariah clerics in American mosques and home-grown radicalization, another with the Muslim Brotherhood network in the U.S.; "Creeping Sharia-ism," which exposes the strategy of imposing Sharia in small steps, which is what we are seeing now; and "Shariah Lawfare," which demonstrates how Islamic law is insinuating itself into the American judicial system on all levels, and not with much resistance from our courts.

(See a recent Jihad Watch article on a legislative initiative in Florida to banish foreign or Sharia law from the state's judiciary. It is just one of several initiatives discussed by Brighton in Chapter 14, "U.S. Representatives and Governors take action: Congressional Hearings and New State Laws.")

One goal of the "stealth," cultural *jihad* in this country by organizations like CAIR, the Muslim Lawyers Association, the Muslim Bar Association of New York, and Muslim Advocates, is to persuade, or browbeat, our judiciary into removing the "foreign" designation from Sharia, and to see it "integrated" into American law as they are now doing in Britain – step by stealthy step. A Telegraph (London) article of March 22nd by John

Bingham, "Islamic law is adopted by British legal chiefs," reports:

Islamic law is to be effectively enshrined in the British legal system for the first time under guidelines for solicitors on drawing up "Sharia compliant" wills.

Under ground-breaking guidance, produced by The Law Society, High Street solicitors will be able to write Islamic wills that deny women an equal share of inheritances and exclude unbelievers altogether. The documents, which would be recognized by Britain's courts, will also prevent children born out of wedlock – and even those who have been adopted – from being counted as legitimate heirs.

Anyone married in a church, or in a civil ceremony, could be excluded from succession under Sharia principles, which recognize only Muslim weddings for inheritance purposes.

Notice how piddly and surreptitious the issues are: Inheritances and wills. Nothing to worry about. The cases will be handled by the British equivalent of American family courts or civil law courts handling suits and torts. It's just some people fussing and feuding over money and custody. None of our business.

The same thing is being attempted here in the U.S. Brighton devotes several pages to the organization American Laws for American Courts (ALAC).

America has unique values of liberty which do not exist in foreign legal systems; this is particularly true in regard to Shariah Islamic Law, included among them, but not limited to the following, are these values and rights: freedom of religion, freedom of speech, freedom of the press, due process, right to privacy, and the right to keep and bear arms.

The goal of the American Laws for American Courts is a clear and unequivocal application of what should be the goal of all state courts: No U.S. citizen or resident should be denied the liberties, rights, and privileges guaranteed in our constitutional republic.

ALAC is a neutral law. it is designed to protect the U.S. Constitutional rights of Americans against any foreign law from any country which challenges their rights. (pp. 224-225)

Some ALAC-style laws were overturned in a few states because they mentioned Islam or Sharia. ALAC then created a draft model law that would not be "country, culture, religion, or ethnic specific." This model seems to have been successful in many states, because neither CAIR nor a dhimmified appellate court could concoct a charge of "Islamophobia" or "discrimination," although the unnamed subject is specifically Islam.

Another hopeful sign is the passage in several states of "anti-libel-tourism" laws that reject foreign suits against Americans accused of libel. The Committee to Protect Journalists features a brief history of those laws, which stemmed from the suit against Rachel Ehrenfeld for publishing a book in 2003 in the U.S., *Funding Evil: How Terrorism is Financed and How to Stop It*, in which she accused billionaire Saudi businessman Khalid bin Mahfouz of channeling funds to terrorist groups.

Ehrenfeld was subsequently sued by Mahfouz in London, but not in the U.S., because the First Amendment protected her. As a consequence, New York passed the appropriately named Libel Terrorism Protection Act in May 2008. It refuses to recognize foreign law, in this instance, Britain's bizarre defamation statutes, and in particular suits brought by super-rich Muslims in other countries.

Chapter 13, "Failure of U.S. leaders to address the threat of Sharia-ism," inadvertently underscores my objection to separating the cream from the milk, that is, making an erroneous distinction between Islam and Sharia law. Islam is one whole cow.

American politicians are fearful of criticizing Islam because it's a "religion," and they don't wish to be accused of attacking *any* religion. This prevents them and now our law-enforcement and intelligence agencies from honestly and effectively addressing the threat posed by Islam. The redaction of all mention of Islam and Muslims from FBI training documents, and the recent dissolution of New York City's crack mosque and Muslim suspect surveillance program by the new socialist mayor of New York (at the behest of Muslim "civil rights" activists) simply blind-sides the country by hamstringing those charged with protecting it from terrorism.

ISIS sex slaves in burqas

A lengthier review of Joy Brighton's book would not do justice to it. Her book is an all-in-one instructive guide to what Islam is, what danger it poses to our country, and what we have and have not done to combat its corrosive "cultural *jihad*" against this country. It names culprits, and it names courageous individuals who have sounded the alarm (often to deaf ears), and lists all the rogues and scoundrels. I think the book is so comprehensive and well done (albeit with my stated reservations above) that a fund should be started to send free copies of it every member of Congress, and also to members of the state legislatures.

There's no vigorish in being a dummy when it comes to betting against Islam. I recommend Brighton's book because it can alert

Americans to the cards – or knives – that are regularly hidden up Islam's sleeve.

Sharia-ism is Here: The Battle to Control Women and Everyone Else, by Joy Brighton. Lexington KY: Sharia-ism Education Center, 2014. 240 pp.

https://edwardcline.blogspot.com/2014/05/sharia-for-dummies.html

Tuesday, May 26, 2015

Chapter 14: Islam in the Academy

**The Kudzu of PC is replacing
the ivy-covered walls of academe**

There is a troika of movements that's coalescing into one ugly phenomenon, a phenomenon that may rival what the world witnessed in the 1930's in Germany. They are a virulent anti-Semitism promoted by the Progressives and the left, its appearance on college campuses and in university classrooms, and the assault on freedom of speech in the guise of being combating "Islamophobia."

A Jihad Watch article of May 23rd, "Campus Watch: Legitimizing Censorship – 'Islamophobia Studies' at Berkeley," by Cinnamon Stillwell and Rima Greene, details the pitiful and organizationally inept efforts of the Islamophobia Research & Documentation Project to pass itself off as a major mover and shaker in the fight against Islamophobia.

"Islamophobia studies" is the latest addition to the academic pantheon of politicized, esoteric, and divisive "studies" whose purpose is to censor criticism of differing views by stigmatizing critics as racist or clinically insane. The University of California, Berkeley's recent Sixth Annual International Islamophobia Conference—organized by the Islamophobia Research & Documentation Project (IRDP)—was titled, "The State of the Islamophobia Studies Field." The fact that this "field" doesn't yet formally exist in the U.S. may explain why speakers the first day of the conference barely mentioned it. As in years past, the conference featured victimology, academic jargon, and anti-Western rhetoric.

The audience, including a number of women in hijabs (headscarves), ranged from twenty to fifty students and faculty members. Because the conference was preempted by another event, it had to shift between two venues. Adding to the confusion, the schedule was made available online only days before. While IRDP director and Near Eastern studies lecturer Hatem Bazian bragged at the outset that the conference livestream had garnered "seven thousand" viewers in 2014, this year, visual and audio problems often rendered it unwatchable.

The spurious audience estimate of between twenty to fifty attendees is a telltale indication that Hatem Bazian was preaching to a miniscule choir, or to a hollow papered hall in which the body count wasn't large enough to absorb the echoes of his words.

In his introduction, Bazian apologized for these mishaps before launching into a glowing report about the alleged state of "Islamophobia studies," which, according to the IRDP website, "has witnessed rapid expansion in the past fifteen years." He claimed that the field had "come of age" in that there is "no longer . . . a debate over whether we should use the term or not" or if "it is real or not," except for "those who really don't want to confront Islamophobia" or "don't want to deal with the reality of what has taken place."

In fact, there is no consensus on the existence of "Islamophobia" in the U.S., particularly in light of FBI statistics showing Jews experiencing the highest number of religiously-motivated hate crimes, with Muslims a distant second. Conflating legitimate criticism of Islam and the myriad human rights abuses occurring in its name all over the world with an irrational fear or prejudice towards all Muslims further obfuscates the matter.

The best way to clean out those library stacks

Bazian claimed that his sparsely attended conference was part of an international series of conferences (but not the OIC, or the Organization of Islam Conferences? How *déclassé*!), spanning the globe from Paris to Switzerland. Stillwell and Greene report, however, that "at this juncture, a search yields no evidence of IRDP-connected conferences this year."

Stillwell and Green then introduce

> Munir Jiwa, founding director of UC Berkeley's Center for Islamic Studies and assistant professor of Islamic studies at the Graduate Theological [*Madrassa*?] Union, followed with the talk, "Frames and Scripts of Islamophobia." Jiwa maintained that the U.S. and the U.K. view Islam through the "frames" of the September 11, 2001 and July 7, 2005 terrorist attacks, respectively, and lamented that, "This forgets the long history of Muslims in the West" and "Muslim contributions to Western civilization." Referring to the alleged shortcomings of the latter—including, ludicrously, the Enlightenment—he made the ahistorical assertion:
>
> *Much like Colonial and Enlightenment ways of dividing the world: us and them. It's as if the West just came up with all these great ideas on its own.*
>
> Jiwa complained that Americans see terrorism as "barbaric," "out of the blue," and "related to Islam," rather than the most warring nation in the world"— i.e., America.

Yes, the U.S. and the U.K. view Islam not only through the "frames" of 9/11 and 7/7, but also through the "frames" of the nearly 26,000 acts of terror worldwide since 9/11 and 7/7. Stillwell and Greene note that Jiwa "never mentioned ISIS's atrocities, only 'our responsibility' in creating the context for that violence."

It's always the victim's fault for creating all those "frames" and "contexts." As soon as we fit them onto a Muslim, he goes ballistic and commits violence, almost as though by auto-suggestion. He's just a pre-programmed automaton, a kind of Pavlovian *cum* Mahometan dog "conditioned" to respond to certain stimuli, such as depictions of Mohammad, or critical or satirical portrayals of Islam. What conditioned him? The anti-mind, anti-reason, anti-life ideology of Islam.

After discussing the Marxist blathering of two other speakers at Bazian's conference, Stillwell and Greene end their article with:

> While this year's conference may have failed to usher in the dawn of an officially recognized "Islamophobia studies," it wasn't for lack of effort. Soon after, IRDP announced the latest edition of its politicized bi-annual publication, the *Islamophobia Studies Journal.* Perhaps following UC Berkeley's lead, Georgetown University recently launched the Bridges Initiative, a project of the Saudi-funded Prince Alwaleed bin Talal Center for Muslim-Christian Understanding devoted to "protecting pluralism – ending Islamophobia."
>
> The subject is all the rage in the field of Middle East studies and throughout academe, which is doing its utmost to silence critics of the Islamic supremacism, systemic social problems, and total chaos plaguing the region. If and when "Islamophobia studies" becomes a reality, we can't claim we didn't see it coming.

It is interesting to note in passing some of the actual funding for "Islamophobia" studies and similar pseudo-academic endeavors. Mike Ciandella wrote in his February 4th, 2014 article for Media Research Center, "$5.6 Million from Soros Aids Universities That Boycott Israel," that:

> The American Studies Association is asking its member universities to join the growing academic

boycott of Israel. Eight out of the 14 member universities of the ASA's National Council that approved the boycott have received more than $5.6 million from George Soros' Open Society Foundations since 2000. The ASA has also been working closely with anti-Israeli organizations to promote this movement.

Promoting anti-Israeli and liberal propaganda, Soros has poured more than $400 million into colleges and universities around the world, including money to most prominent institutions in the United States. According to a May 2012 article in The New York Times, Soros gave $500,000 a year to J Street, a "two-state solution" organization whose co-founder, Daniel Levy, called the creation of Israel in 1948 "an act that was wrong." Some of the $23.8 million that Soros has given to Bard College in New York has gone to a Palestinian youth group, and Bard also offers joint degree programs at a Palestinian school in Jerusalem, and partners closely with Al-Quds University.

According to the ASA, this boycott is part of the larger BDS, or "Boycott, Divestment and Sanctions" movement. BDS promotes the work of Hamas and Hezbollah, as well as arguing for a "one-state solution" to the Israeli/Palestinian conflict, which would involve Palestinians having equal right of return status in Israel with Israelis.

I always chuckle when I read that Soros's "Open Society" machine is involved in one or another program to "transform" America into a "more tolerant democracy." It's a risible misnomer, when what Soros and his winged monkeys have in mind in the end is a *closed society* – closed to freedom of thought and to freedom of speech.

The official <u>BDS site</u> encourages the academic boycott of Israel:

> The Palestinian Campaign for the Academic and Cultural Boycott of Israel (PACBI) was one of the founding entities in 2005 of the Palestinian Civil Society BDS Campaign and remains a key part of the Palestinian-led, global BDS movement.
>
> PACBI was launched in Ramallah in April 2004 by a group of Palestinian academics and intellectuals to join the growing international boycott movement. The Campaign built on the Palestinian call for a **comprehensive economic, cultural and academic boycott of Israel** issued in August 2002 and a statement made by Palestinian academics and intellectuals in the occupied territories and in the Diaspora calling for a boycott of Israeli academic institutions in October 2003....
>
> The PACBI Call states:
> "We, Palestinian academics and intellectuals, call upon our colleagues in the international community to *comprehensively and consistently boycott all Israeli academic and cultural institutions* as a contribution to the struggle to end Israel's occupation, colonization and system of apartheid, by applying the following:

1. Refrain from participation in any form of academic and cultural cooperation, collaboration or joint projects with Israeli institutions;
2. Advocate a comprehensive boycott of Israeli institutions at the national and international levels, including suspension of all forms of funding and subsidies to these institutions;
3. Promote divestment and disinvestment from Israel by international academic institutions;

4. Work toward the condemnation of Israeli policies by pressing for resolutions to be adopted by academic, professional and cultural associations and organizations;

5. Support Palestinian academic and cultural institutions directly without requiring them to partner with Israeli counterparts as an explicit or implicit condition for such support."

In academia – on the physical campuses, in the ivy that clings to their walls but which is infested with the black widow spiders of Marxism, and in the suffocating, light-dimming canopies of culturally diverse kudzu – this agenda will manifest itself into active anti-Semitism of the violent kind. Boycotting Israeli goods and thinkers and speakers and associations translates into anti-Semitism. There isn't any other meaning possible.

**Christians and Muslims both have
a long history of book burning.**

Being an Israeli is synonymous with being Jewish, even though one may be an atheist or a Christian or an Arab-Israeli Muslim, you're still "Jewish" and can be "boycotted" or bashed in the face or beaten up or even murdered. You're still an "occupier" of Palestinian land and a racist and a colonizer over the bodies the Palestinian children and a ruthless oppressor of Palestinian workers. The Boycott, Divestment, and Sanction movement against Israel means business, and isn't limited to a tenured professor flapping his gums about the outrages committed by Israelis, or to half-witted slobs sporting keffryahs and niqabs carrying signs and shouting themselves hoarse, "Brains dead! Don't shoot!"

While the BDS crowd keeps boasting of how it helped to end apartheid in South Africa, it equates that with trying to end "apartheid" in Israel. I've seen no recent calls by that crowd to protest oppression, exploitation, and discrimination in Saudi Arabia, Red China, Zimbabwe, Iran, North Korea, Libya, Egypt, Yemen, and other sundry dictatorships and authoritarian countries. It's only against tiny Israel, the freest and most prosperous country in the Middle East.

The American Studies Association has been recruiting universities to join in BDS and to become signatories of the BDS Resolution of December 2013 to boycott Israeli academic institutions. The ASA, founded in 1951 and purportedly "the oldest scholarly organization devoted to the interdisciplinary study of American culture and history," has been captured by the Left and is now apparently devoted to imposing a politically correct discipline. The Jerusalem Post of January 1st, 2014, reported, however, that ninety-two universities rejected the academic boycott of Israel.

> More than 90 American universities have so far released statements rejecting the American Studies Association decision to boycott Israeli academic institutions, and several have cut ties with the organization in protest.
>
> The Conference of Presidents of Major American Jewish Organizations expressed appreciation to university presidents and chancellors who "stood up against this discriminatory and unjustified measure and rejected the ASA boycott of Israel."

But not all is well with the university and education heads. Many of them belong to what Salman Rushdie, who still lives with an Iranian fatwa on his head, might have called the "But…Brigade" when it came to endorsing freedom of speech. "We're for freedom of speech, but…." Or perhaps these hypersensitive folk should be called "Butt-Heads."

> Molly Corbett, president of the American Council on Education – an umbrella group that covers 1,800 institutions and claims to be the "most visible and influential higher education association" in the US – issued a statement on Sunday that "such actions are *misguided* and greatly troubling, as they strike at the heart of academic freedom….
>
> We hope the leadership of these organizations [who support the boycott] soon reconsiders their actions and trust that other scholarly organizations will see the troubling implications of such boycotts and avoid [a] similar vote…." [brackets mine]

Misguided? But BDS is nothing if not clear and on-target about its means and ends. To call the ends of BDS – one of which is the economic submission and eventual destruction of Israel – "misguided" is like calling an armed hold-up a "misguided" attempt to augment one's income.

> Princeton president Christopher L. Eisgruber dubbed the boycott "misguided," adding that singling Israel out was "indefensible."
>
> But while Eisgruber noted that his "personal support for scholarly engagement with Israel is enthusiastic and unequivocal," he said he did not intend to denounce the ASA or cut Princeton's institutional ties with the organization.
>
> "My hope is that the ASA 's more thoughtful and

reasonable members will eventually bring the organization to its senses – here, too, engagement may be better than a boycott," he wrote.

But the central method of BDS is to bypass thought and reason and to rely on emotion and a virulent strain of anti-Semitism to accomplish its ends. There are no "thoughtful and reasonable" members in BDS. The only "engagement" they're interested in is violence and force and censorship.

A May 4th article by Ruth Wisse in Mosaic Magazine, "Anti-Semitism Goes to School," reveals the depth of the anti-Israel sentiment and of the anti-Semitism.

> In February, a Jewish college student was hospitalized after being punched in the face at a pro-Palestinian demonstration on a campus in upstate New York. His family has insisted on maintaining the boy's privacy, but other such incidents, some caught on camera, include a male student punched in the face at Temple University, a female student at Ohio University harassed for defending Israel, and a male student at Cornell threatened physically for protesting anti-Israel propaganda. On three successive days last summer, the Boston police had to protect a student rally for Israel from pro-Palestinian mobs shouting "Jews back to Birkenau!" At the University of California-Irvine, this year's Israel Independence Day festivities were blocked and shouted down by anti-Israel demonstrators. Every year, some 200 campuses now host a multiday hate-the-Jews fest, its malignancy encapsulated in its title: "Israel Apartheid Week…."

> Nor are students the only targets. At Connecticut College, to cite but the most recent example, a quietly pro-Israel professor of philosophy has been

maliciously singled out and hounded as a "racist" in a campaign instigated by Palestinian activists, endorsed by numerous faculty members, and at least tacitly complied with by the college administration and the campus Hillel organization. At the annual meetings of prestigious academic associations, boycott resolutions against Israel and Israeli academic institutions are routinely aired and often passed.

Wisse's article is long and detailed in her examination of the anti-Israel phenomenon in this country, and is worth reading in its entirety. Some highlights are:

As one of its first acts in December 1945, the Arab League called on all Arab institutions and individuals to refuse to deal in, distribute, or consume Jewish and Zionist products or manufactured goods. Seventy years later, calls for boycott of Israel, under the acronym BDS—boycott, divestment, and sanctions—have become a staple of American university agendas, extending not only to Israeli companies like Soda Stream but to Israeli scholars in the humanities and social sciences. Last year, a petition by "anthropologists for the boycott of Israeli academic institutions" garnered the signatures of the relevant department chairs at (among others) Harvard, Wesleyan, and San Francisco State. The American Studies Association attracted the "largest number of participants in the organization's history" for a vote endorsing a boycott of Israeli academic institutions.

Keep in mind that the briefly described incidents here did not occur in Nazi Germany:

....Which is not to say that grounds are lacking for larger concern. In addition to the catalog of academic offenses I've briefly summarized here, a growing number of anti-Jewish incidents—from a swastika-desecrated Jewish cemetery in New Jersey to fatal shootings at a Kansas City Jewish community center—has been registered by agencies like the Anti-Defamation League and the American Jewish Committee. At the government level, more ominously, and perhaps for the first time in recent American history, it is the White House, rather than the once notoriously Arabist State Department, that has taken the lead in threatening to isolate the Jewish state. President Obama's frankly contemptuous treatment of Israel's prime minister smacks more of the university than of the Senate in which he once served, but he *is* the president, and his words and actions give license to others.

The linkages between the assault on American values and on Jews is not so complex that it needs lengthy explication. To wit:

Contrary to the claims of administrators like the chancellor of UCLA, prosecuting the war against the Jews is not an issue of free speech, "sacrosanct to any university campus." Had UCLA's chancellor and president faced a campaign to reinstate segregation, recriminalize homosexuality, or bar women from the faculty club, they would have reacted with more than "concern." Yet behind the banner of free speech, they tolerate, however squeamishly, campaigns to undo the Jewish homeland and to demonize the already most mythified people on earth. Anti-Jewish politics are no more innocent when pursued by left-wing American SOCCs and SOOPs than when they were prosecuted by right-wing European blackshirts [*sic*]....

Indeed, institutions that enforce "sensitivity training" to insure toleration for gays, blacks, and other minorities may inadvertently be bringing some of these groups together in common hostility to Jews as the only campus minority against whom hostility is *condoned*. On almost every campus in the land, the norms of political correctness are rigorously enforced; punitive speech codes proliferate; a phalanx of administrative functionaries labors so that nothing said, or read, will ever offend the sensibilities of any student— with one licensed exception. Multiculturalism has found its apotheosis in a multicultural coalition of anti-Zionists: a uniquely constituted political phenomenon with its own functions, strategies, and goals.

I have a hypothesis about anti-Semitism and Jew hatred on or off campus. It is probably not even an original hypothesis. It is based on nothing more disgusting and damning than *envy*. When you recall all the accomplishments of Jewish men and women over the centuries – in scholarship, in science, in finance, in business, in the arts – what is it that Jews are most resented and hated for? What they've done in the face of persecution, genocide, and pointed discrimination when they were not being persecuted, punished, or murdered.

Writing as an atheist who is beholden to no religion, I am naturally confounded by the attraction to or loyalty to Judaism. I could poke holes in it as easily as I can poke holes in Islam and Catholicism or in any other species of Christianity or faith. What I see, however, in the BDS movement and in the poison ivy-covered halls and walls of academe is racism – even among those self-hating Jews who lend their hands to BDS and to all manner of anti-Israel causes. The latter really need to book themselves some time on a therapist's couch to thrash out that self-hatred. It's a unique pathology; I haven't read about self-hating

Episcopalians calling for the dismemberment and downfall of the Anglican Church.

Is Judaism a "race"? I think not. Neither is Islam. I wouldn't know a Jew on the street unless he was wearing a sandwich board or a kippa.

BDS and anti-Semitism are birds of the same diseased feather. What is perhaps most important is that BDS and anti-Semitism in the schools is simply that their horrendous maledictions against Israel and Jews enable Islam to insert itself into the phenomena and eventually reach a terms-setting ascendency. That is already happening in an incremental, stealthy progression in American education at all levels, and bodes no good for freedom of speech.

https://edwardcline.blogspot.com/2015/05/islam-in-academy.html

Monday, September 19, 2016

Chapter 15: A Stew Pot of Notable News

You can tolerate a little rape, can't you? Start tolerance!

I could not pass this up. It is one of the dumbest, most politically correct, and insulting pro-immigration ads that has passed my desk. It has appeared on German TV. Paul Joseph Watson reports on Infowars:

> A television ad currently airing in Germany invites blonde-haired, blue-eyed women to embrace "tolerance" by wearing the Muslim hijab head dress.

> The commercial begins with the text "Turkish women wear the hijab," as a veiled woman is seen with her back to the camera.

> However, when she turns around it immediately becomes clear that the woman is a white, blonde-haired German, before she states, "Me too! It's beautiful!"

> "Enjoy difference – start tolerance," states the woman.

The campaign is funded by the United Nations
Educational, Scientific and Cultural Organization,
as well as German taxpayers, who are forced to
obtain a state television license or face prison time.

Instead of reversing its suicidal immigration policy, it appears as
though Germany is now encouraging its female population to
avoid the mass sex assaults committed by Muslim migrants in
numerous major cities by submitting to Islam and covering
themselves up.

The outfit worn by the model is about as Sharia compliant as a
Halloween gypsy costume you might see at a college sorority
party. Frankly, it is quite fetching. It is distinctly *not* Turkish or
any style resembling approved Islamic norms. The woman is *not*
wearing a hair-covering hijab. It is definitely an invitation to
rape, as she is decidedly "uncovered meat," to judge by Sharia
measures of "modesty."

If any woman appeared in Germany (or in France, or in Sweden,
or in any Muslim conquered or invaded Continental country) in
that kind of outfit she would be immediately surrounded by
Muslim men, groped, and thrown to the ground and given the
Lara Logan Cairo treatment. The costume would be ripped from
her body. Then she could "enjoy the difference" and do her bit in
"enjoying tolerance." Right? If she complained, she could be
punished by Merkel's tolerance police and accused of "racism"
or "Islamophobia." *"You did not start tolerance!"* they'd shout.

You have to ask yourself what possessed the minds of the
producers of the ad to turn out such a putrid piece of propaganda.
Well, it could not have been sanity. Speaking of Turkish dress,
Turks in Germany are especially brutal as they like to disfigure
their European victims after the gang rapes. I've only seen
Turkish belly dancers so attired in movies.

130

Please note that it is not Muslims or any of those Muslim male adult "refugees" who are being asked to "start tolerance," although they may, as criminals, "enjoy the difference" in the act of sexual assault. It is German women who are being urged to submit to Islam by voluntarily covering themselves up and staying out of sight. I would be as welcome to an Obama or Hillary Clinton rally dressed as Uncle Sam or sporting a "Make America Great Again" cap. A German woman would stand a similar chance of non-molestation in any Muslim "no-go" neighborhood. I'd be beaten up by #Never Trump morons and social justice warrior thugs.

On another front, "refugee" champion George Clooney, who owns about a dozen million-dollar mansions around the world, including at Lake Como, Italy, is reluctant to allow migrants anywhere near that personal refuge from reality. As with other members of the establishment "elite," Clooney wishes to insulate himself from the destructive consequences of his policies. Dealing with the rapes, robberies, and other culturally "enriching" habits of savages is not for him, just for the *hoi polloi*, otherwise known as the "deplorables." Hillary Clinton unintentionally handed Donald Trump the perfect meme by calling his supporters "a basket case of deplorables."

Tolerance for thee, but not for me.

Breitbart reported on July 13th:

The migration of hundreds of people from Arab nations, Africa, and Asia was triggered following the Swiss government's decision to close its southern border with Italy.

Now, waiting for smugglers to lead them into northern Europe, groups of migrants are camping out in tattered tents around the Lake Como resort.

Flimsy dwellings, clothes and trash are scattered around the Northern Italian town's railway station, where dozens of new families and refugees have flocked....

The migrant camp is, oddly enough, just steps away from the front door of immigration activists' George and Amal Clooney's multi-million dollar lakeside mansion in Lake Como, according to the *Daily Mail*.

The couple was recently pictured drinking tequila while watching fireworks on a boat near the property alongside their close friend Bill Murray.

The Clooneys have taken refuge from the Hollywood spotlight in their summer home in Italy for years. Last year, *Page Six* reported that Clooney was mulling putting his Lake Como villa on the market due to ever-present and intrusive paparazzi.

It is unclear if the recent deluge of refugees pouring into town will have an affect on Clooney's decision to sell or not.

The power couple has spent some time talking about the migrant crisis. The Clooneys met privately with German Chancellor Angela Merkel in

> February and praised and thanked her for her
> leadership during the crisis....
>
> George has previously described Trump as a
> "xenophobic fascist" who wants to "ban Muslims
> from the country."

I guess Clooney is hoping we don't label him as a "xenophobic fascist," as well, for thinking about selling his Lake Como mansion to put some distance between him and his adopted "children." No, we won't call him that. Instead, we'll call him a hypocritical pull-peddler and social justice warrior who is reluctant to rub shoulders with the "refugees" or risk having Amal groped or worse by other culture "enrichers."

> Amal Clooney, the British-Lebanese human rights
> attorney who married George in 2014, slammed
> Republican presumptive presidential nominee
> Donald Trump this past April, saying his
> immigration stance and promise to build a wall on
> the Mexican border do not represent "U.S. values."

George and Amal know as much about "U.S. values" as I do about phrenology or dialectical materialism.

We, the MSM, don't need no stinkin' objectivity!

That also goes for the MSM. It has abandoned all pretense of reporting any news concerning Donald Trump and Hillary Clinton and adopted a "what we say goes" philosophy of slander and puffery. It may not pass as "truth," but who's to say what truth is? It's whatever we want it to be, and if you don't believe it then you're a racist, xenophobic, anti-Islam pig. Never mind that Hillary is sodden with corruption, chargeable felonious offenses, and treason, we, the MSM, believe she knows all about "U.S. values" and we want this beast to sit in the White House and guide this country to the oblivion it so richly deserves, to continue the destruction implemented by Barack Obama. We stick our tongues out at objectivity and truth.

Justin Raimondo of the LA Times reported in his August 2nd article, "To fight Trump, journalists have dispensed with objectiviity." He asks:

> Why are the rules of journalism being rewritten this election year?
>
> This transparent bias is a national phenomenon, infecting both print and television media to such an extent that it has become almost impossible to separate coverage of the Trump campaign from attempts to tear it down. The media has long been accused of having a liberal slant, but in this cycle journalists seem to have cast themselves as defenders of the republic against what they see as a major threat, and in playing this role they've lost the ability to assess events rationally....
>
> To take a recent example: Trump said at a news conference that he hoped the Russians — who are accused of hacking the Democratic National Committee's computers — would release the 30,000 emails previously erased by Clinton's staff. The DNC went ballistic, claiming that Trump had asked the Russians to commit "espionage" against

the United States. Aside from the fact that Trump was obviously joking, Clinton claims those emails, which were on her unauthorized server during her tenure as secretary of State, were about her yoga lessons and personal notes to her husband — so how would revealing them endanger "national security"? Yet the media reported this accusation uncritically. A New York Times piece by Maggie Haberman and Ashley Parker, ostensibly reporting Trump's contention that he spoke in jest, nonetheless averred that "the Republican nominee basically urged Russia, an adversary, to conduct cyber-espionage against a former secretary of state." Would it be a stretch to conclude from this description that the New York Times is a Trump adversary?

Polls shows that journalism is one of the least respected professions in the country, and with Trump calling out media organizations for their bias, widespread slanted reporting is bound to reinforce this point — and to backfire. Trump's campaign is throwing down the gauntlet to the political class. If journalists are seen as the mouthpiece of that class, they may soon find themselves covering Trump's inauguration.

Raimondo concludes that his local newspaper, the Sonoma County Press-Democrat, "is   clearly in the tank for Hillary Clinton," and that can be said as well for the rest of the MSM.

**Sheep that could not recite
the Shahada, had its throat cut.**

In the meantime, Barack Obama wants us all to "enjoy the difference" and help Muslims in America celebrate Eid al-Adha, the "holiday" when Muslims butcher animals by slitting their throats and letting them bleed to death in agony. It's a religion, don't you see? It's *halal*. It's culturally "enriching."

He said, on September 12th, to help "commemorate" 9/11:

> "We are reminded of the millions of refugees around the globe who are spending this sacred holiday separated from their families, unsure of their future, but still hoping for a brighter tomorrow," Mr. Obama said in a statement. "And as a nation, we remain committed to welcoming the stranger with empathy and an open heart — from the refugee who flees war-torn lands to the immigrant who leaves home in search of a better life."
>
> Eid al-Adha, also known as the Festival of the Sacrifice, began Sunday night and ends Thursday night.

I wonder who really wrote that. Angela Merkel? George Clooney? Hillary Clinton? Loretta Lynch? You see, there is no difference between *halal* butchery of animals and what ISIS and other Islamic Justice Warriors have done to or wish to do to all Jews and infidels: slit their throats and let them bleed to death.

Remember how the stewardesses and pilots of the 9/11 planes died with those boxcutters? That's *halal*.

https://edwardcline.blogspot.com/2016/09/a-stew-pot-of-notable-news.html

Wednesday, July 22, 2015

Chapter 16: The Moderate Muslim Moonie

A Muslim or a Moonie in prayerful selflessness? What's the difference –
except in the one creed's 14-century-old homicide record?

Mohammad: "Upon this rock I will bang my head."

Reading Robert Spencer's PJ Media article of July 1th, "Chattanooga Shooter Marinated in Self-Pity Over 'Islamophobia,'" and Pamela Geller's Atlas Shrugs article, "Chattanooga Jihadi's Anti-American Diary: Wanted to be a Suicide Martyr for Islam" of July 20th, I was struck by the similarities between the empty vessel that was Muhammad Youssef Abdulazeez and the average Moonie.

What is a Moonie?

A Moonie is a member of the Unification Church of the United States, a religious or cult-like movement that was imported to the U.S. from South Korea by the Rev. Sun Myung Moon (1920-2012). Here is some background on Moon and his religion.

> When he was 15 years old [in 1935], at Easter, he believes that Jesus Christ appeared to him in a vision, charging him with the responsibility of completing the work in the world that Jesus had started. During his adult life he has had trouble with legal authorities, having been arrested for practicing capitalism (a crime in North Korea),

charged (but not convicted) in South Korea of
other activities, and convicted of tax evasion in the
United States. During 1948, the *Presbyterian
Church of Korea* felt that his views were
incompatible with traditional Christianity; they
excommunicated him.

If you thought Islam had a bizarre and utterly irrational set of
tenets, try on the Unification Church's for size.

While many of the beliefs of the Unification Church
are identical to those of other conservative Christian
groups, there are some major differences:

They view God as a single being with *"perfect
intellect, emotion and will."* They reject the
traditional Christian concept of the Trinity. God
contains within himself positive (male) and negative
(female) aspects, which are in perfect harmony with
each other.

This is basically Islam's Allah but without the transgendering.
The Moonie God can also know everything, and be able to do
anything, any time. It's the old omniscience vs. omnipotence
card trick. However, I don't recall in my Islamic readings that
Allah was said to possess an intellect, perfect or imperfect. After
all, if you can know everything, and do anything, at any time,
you really don't need an intellect, do you? That is, you don't
need to think. You don't need to posit an argument for why
everyone should bow and scrape to you. You just say, "Fear me,
or else you' burn in hell forever and ever. Fear me, and obey me,
and I'll reward you with 72 raisins and all the Kickapoo juice you
want forever and ever."

The Holy Spirit is the feminine counterpart to God. She is not a
person, but is a form of energy that is derived from God.

In Christianity the Holy Ghost is represented by a white dove. Which is just a glorified pigeon.

There's some folderol about Eve first having an affair with Lucifer, and then a roll in the hay with Adam – before they were even married! Both episodes with the skank Eve contributed to the physical and spiritual fall of mankind. The Unification Church puts much stress on celibacy until the marrying age. Teenage sex is a non-no.

There are other bizarre tenets, but the chief one is that Jesus was executed before he could complete his work and before he got married. When he returns at the End of Days, he will reign over an earth that is Paradise and he *will* marry.

> God's original intent was for Jesus Christ to form a perfect marriage in order to redeem humanity, and undo the harm perpetrated by Adam and Eve. Since Jesus was executed before accomplishing his mission, it will be up to a third Adam in the present day to form this perfect marriage and complete Jesus' task.

Like Islam, sex and women have important roles in Moonie-ism. Women are still second-class citizens in Moonie-ism, but they aren't the natural subjects of beatings, rape, polygamy, and the whole "walk behind me" tradition to be found in Islam. Also, in Moonie-ism female garb isn't prescribed. Bikinis may be optional.

Finally, the Unification Church has its own version of the Thirteenth Imam, the one who's supposed to herald the End of Days and send everyone rushing to queue up for a trip to Paradise or Hell.

> They believe that the third Adam was born in Korea between 1917 and 1930. (The first Adam was the individual described in Genesis; the second Adam is

Jesus). The third Adam will be recognized as the second coming of Christ, the perfect man. He will marry the perfect woman, and will become the *"true spiritual parents of humankind"*. Many members of the Unification Church regard Rev. Moon and his second (and current) wife Hak Ja Han as these parents.

This puts Moon in the running as being Moonie-ism's own "prophet Mohammad," as well. I have no idea whom the Moonies regard now as the Third Adam since the original Moon died from pneumonia in 2012. The thrust of this column is that, like Islam, Moonie-ism requires a certain degree of selflessness in an individual to join the movement, together with a level of gullibility that hovers near clinically defined imbecility.

One chief difference between Moonie-ism and Islam is that most Muslims are born into their religious environment and so their minds are "captured" by the ideology before they can even begin to think about whether or not it makes any sense. Still, they choose to remain "captured." Being born into an insane religion and ideology and not thinking about it doesn't let the average, Friday-go-to-prayers Muslim and convenience store operator off the hook for passively accepting the same ideology in whose name his more obsessed and activist brothers kill and destroy. "Moderate" Muslims come a dime a dozen. But then so did "moderate" Nazis and "moderate" Communists and "moderate" Shintoists All three of the latter creeds produced brutal armies of adherents.

The Moonies have not. Muslims can coast along quietly in their creed and make a show of clucking their tongues publicly at the depredations of their rampaging religious brethren. Moonies can also stand at the sidelines when the latest child abuse scandal brings down some Catholic clerics.

But they don't form armies or wear suicide vests or march on cities or villages or invade editorial offices and slaughter the staff.

Most Moonies, however, choose to become Moonies. They're not mentally enfeebled. Dysfunctional in terms of their epistemology and metaphysics, yes. They make that choice in their teens or early adulthood after living in the real world and perhaps even after having attained a level of financial success (the Rev. Moon required converts to sign over their wealth to him or to the church.) Converting to Moonie-ism required an abject surrender of one's self *and* one's livelihood. They are looking for something "greater" than themselves (thanks to the ubiquitous morality of altruism in the culture) to "belong" to.

The average Muslim is a *maquette*
who is comfortable with a group identity and is
unwilling or unable to venture beyond
the group, either from fear of retribution or
from just plain mental inertia

More importantly for Moonies is the desire to belong to a religion that is basically *counter-culture*. They convince themselves that all the established churches (and perhaps even Judaism) are weak institutions corrupted by the hand of Satan. The Moonie wants to believe he "belongs" to a purer manifestation of Christ's teachings. That makes him exceptional. It gives him a sense of self, counterfeit though it may be. And he's not supposed to feel proud about it. Pride is not a virtue in

Moonie-ism just as it isn't in Islam, except if you've beheaded an infidel or raped a Yazidi.

The highpoint of a Muslim's existence is *non-existence*, when his "soul" is merged with the Islamic *Ummah*, an ethereal entity that includes *all* Muslims.

One can almost forgive Muslims for being what they are, abject servants of Allah's will. Muslims are taught to be selfless from day one. Moonies, thinking they're not altruistic enough, want to be more selfless than they already may be. Muslims are taught from childhood on that they are nothing here on earth but instruments of Allah's grand plan. Selflessness and service to the *Umma* (the global Muslim "community") is a core virtue.

I think many Americans who today convert to Islam would have converted to the Unification Church in its heyday. As with Islam, Moonie-ism doesn't require much thought to be devout and staying the righteous path to God's or Allah's good graces. All it requires is an unquestioning capacity for belief in any old wives' tale or Tales from the Crypt or the benevolent episodes from the riotous life of Mohammad, together with a companion capacity for unreserved obedience.

Moonies have been known to be de-programmed and released from captivity from Moonie-ism. De-programmers intervene and bring them to their senses. As Steven Hassan, a former leader in the Unification Church said in a Guardian article – and this substantiates the charge that Moonie-ism required individuals to become committed and selfless:

> Within three months I was a cult leader. I got very deeply involved, and I got to the point where I was being told to think about what country I wanted to run when we took over the world.
>
> I was with the Moonies for two-and-a-half years. I worked 21 hours a day, seven days a week – in

prayer for between one and three hours. Then I
would spend the rest of the day doing PR or lectures
for the group, recruiting and fundraising. Everyone
on my team was told they had to raise a minimum
of $100 a day, otherwise they wouldn't be allowed
to sleep, and as a good leader, if they couldn't sleep,
then I couldn't either. When I crashed a van into the
back of a tractor trailer, I had gone three days
without sleep.

Hassan said in his Guardian article that "people don't knowingly
join cults." Oh, but they do, if the cult fits their particular brand
of selflessness.

The only means of salvation of a Moonie must be initiated by
parents, relatives or friends. It means sessions of de-
programming. Randall Watters has some interesting information
on how to rescue a Moonie from the clutches of the Unification
Church.

Can Muslims be de-programmed? Not in the usual sense. Many
of the most outspoken critics of Islam have been ex-Muslims:
Ayaan Hirsi Ali, Walid Shoebat, Bosch Fawstin, Salman
Rushdie, and dozens of others. But such de-programming has
been largely self-initiated when an individual allows his
rationality to delve into the "mysteries" and "internal
contradictions" of Islam. His rational faculties were not so much
corroded by mysticism as crippled. Being merely crippled, the
individual was able to get back up on his feet and take action.

But your average, non-thinking Muslim has been psychologically
immunized against reason. He has zero tolerance for it and
doesn't even know it. The irrational, he's been told by Islam, is
in the natural order of things. If Allah isn't merciful or allows
awful things to happen, that's in the way of his "grand plan"
which is incomprehensible to mere mortals burdened with reason
and the evidence of their senses. Christian apologists also cite a

similar indemnification and disclaimer for God when it comes to explaining tidal waves that wipe out thousands, erupting volcanoes that wipe out whole towns, and ISIS wiping out whole towns of Christians in the Middle East.

Islam and Moonie-ism have no use for a complete man, only for human *maquettes* like Muhammad Youssef Abdulazeez.

https://edwardcline.blogspot.com/2015/07/the-moderate-muslim-moonie.html

Thursday, July 28, 2016

Chapter 17: The Destructiveness of Political Correctness

A guest essay by William S. Lind from An Accuracy in Academia Association meeting in 1998. The Wikipedia entry for him reads:

William S. Lind (born July 9, 1947) is an American monarchist, paleoconservative, columnist, Christian, and a light rail enthusiast. He's the author of several books and one of the first proponents of the Fourth-generation warfare theory. More recently Lind has advocated for police to have RPGs as standard issue, and for a return to death by hanging as a common sentence for crime in 'urban areas.' Lind is a key proponent of the "Cultural Marxism" conspiracy theory, he asserts that Marxists control much of modern popular media, and that Political correctness can be directly attributed to Karl Marx. Lind also wrote *Victoria: A Novel of 4th Generation War*, in which a group of Christian Marines leads an armed rebellion against political correctness within the American government. He revealed using the pseudonym Thomas Hobbes in a column for *The American Conservative*.

See also the Full Wikipedia on Lind. Here is his ALA paper on political correctness:

The Origins of Political Correctness

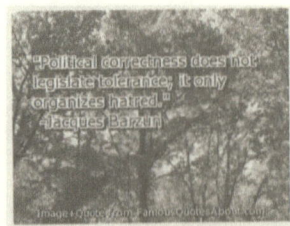

An observation from the late, great Barzun

Variations of this speech have been delivered to various AIA conferences including the 2000 Conservative University at American University

Where does all this stuff that you've heard about this morning – the victim feminism, the gay rights movement, the invented statistics, the rewritten history, the lies, the demands, all the rest of it – where does it come from? For the first time in our history, Americans have to be fearful of what they say, of what they write, and of what they think. They have to be afraid of using the wrong word, a word denounced as offensive or insensitive, or racist, sexist, or homophobic.

We have seen other countries, particularly in this century, where this has been the case. And we have always regarded them with a mixture of pity, and to be truthful, some amusement, because it has struck us as so strange that people would allow a situation to develop where they would be afraid of what words they used. But we now have this situation in this country. We have it primarily on college campuses, but it is spreading throughout the whole society. Were does it come from? What is it?

We call it "Political Correctness." The name originated as something of a joke, literally in a comic strip, and we tend still to think of it as only half-serious. In fact, it's deadly serious. It is the great disease of our century, the disease that has left tens of millions of people dead in Europe, in Russia, in China, indeed around the world. It is the disease of ideology. PC is not funny. PC is deadly serious.

If we look at it analytically, if we look at it historically, we quickly find out exactly what it is. Political Correctness is cultural Marxism. It is Marxism translated from economic into cultural terms. It is an effort that goes back not to the 1960s and the hippies and the peace movement, but back to World War I. If we compare the basic tenets of Political Correctness with classical Marxism the parallels are very obvious.

*

First of all, both are totalitarian ideologies. The totalitarian nature of Political Correctness is revealed nowhere more clearly than on college campuses, many of which at this point are small ivy covered North Koreas, where the student or faculty member who dares to cross any of the lines set up by the gender feminist or the homosexual-rights activists, or the local black or Hispanic group, or any of the other sainted "victims" groups that PC revolves around, quickly find themselves in judicial trouble. Within the small legal system of the college, they face formal charges – some star-chamber proceeding – and punishment. That is a little look into the future that Political Correctness intends for the nation as a whole.

**And we plan to have
many more spoiled brats!**

Indeed, all ideologies are totalitarian because the essence of an ideology (I would note that conservatism correctly understood is not an ideology) is to take some philosophy and say on the basis of this philosophy certain things must be true – such as the whole of the history of our culture is the history of the oppression of women. Since reality contradicts that, reality must be forbidden. It must become forbidden to acknowledge the reality of our history. People must be forced to live a lie, and since people are naturally reluctant to live a lie, they naturally use their ears and eyes to look out and say, "Wait a minute. This isn't true. I can see it isn't true," the power of the state must be put behind the demand to live a lie. That is why ideology invariably creates a totalitarian state.

Second, the cultural Marxism of Political Correctness, like economic Marxism, has a single factor explanation of history. Economic Marxism says that all of history is determined by ownership of means of production. Cultural Marxism, or Political Correctness, says that all history is determined by power, by which groups defined in terms of race, sex, etc., have power over which other groups. Nothing else matters. All literature, indeed, is about that. Everything in the past is about that one thing.

Third, just as in classical economic Marxism certain groups, i.e. workers and peasants, are a priori good, and other groups, i.e., the bourgeoisie and capital owners, are evil. In the cultural Marxism of Political Correctness certain groups are good – feminist women, (only feminist women, non-feminist women are deemed not to exist) blacks, Hispanics, homosexuals. These groups are determined to be "victims," and therefore automatically good regardless of what any of them do. Similarly, white males are determined automatically to be evil, thereby becoming the equivalent of the bourgeoisie in economic Marxism.

Fourth, both economic and cultural Marxism rely on expropriation. When the classical Marxists, the communists, took over a country like Russia, they expropriated the bourgeoisie, they took away their property. Similarly, when the cultural Marxists take over a university campus, they expropriate through things like quotas for admissions. When a white student with superior qualifications is denied admittance to a college in favor of a black or Hispanic who isn't as well qualified, the white student is expropriated. And indeed, affirmative action, in our whole society today, is a system of expropriation. White owned companies don't get a contract because the contract is reserved for a company owned by, say, Hispanics or women. So expropriation is a principle tool for both forms of Marxism.

And finally, both have a method of analysis that automatically gives the answers they want. For the classical Marxist, it's Marxist economics. For the cultural Marxist, it's instant deconstruction.

Deconstruction essentially takes any text, removes all meaning from it and re-inserts any meaning desired. So we find, for example, that all of Shakespeare is about the suppression of women, or the Bible is really about race and gender. All of these texts simply become grist for the mill, which proves that "all history is about which groups have power over which other groups." So the parallels are very evident between the classical Marxism that we're familiar with in the old Soviet Union and the cultural Marxism that we see today as Political Correctness.

https://edwardcline.blogspot.com/2016/07/on-destructiveness-of-political.html

www.ingramcontent.com/pod-product-compliance
Lightning Source LLC
Chambersburg PA
CBHW020518290526
45786CB00002B/652